THE

THE PIPE BOOK

ALFRED DUNHILL

PREFACE BY RICHARD DUNHILL

SKYHORSE PUBLISHING

Skyhorse Publishing books may be purchased in bulk at special discounts for sales promotion, corporate gifts, fund-raising, or educational purposes. Special editions can also be created to specifications. For details, contact the Special Sales Department, Skyhorse Publishing, 307 West 36th Street, 11th Floor, New York, NY 10018 or info@skyhorsepublishing.com.

Skyhorse® and Skyhorse Publishing® are registered trademarks of Skyhorse Publishing, Inc.®, a Delaware corporation.

www.skyhorsepublishing.com

10 9 8 7 6 5 4 3 2 1

Library of Congress Cataloging-in-Publication Data is available on file.

ISBN: 978-1-61608-049-5

Printed in the United States of America

PREFACE

The story of *The Pipe Book* cannot be told separately from the story of the company Alfred Dunhill Limited. Like most companies, ours had a romantic beginning.

Alfred Dunhill, my grandfather, was born on 30 September 1872 in Hornsey, north of London. Henry Dunhill, his father, operated a piano warehouse as well as a sack-making business, which expanded while Alfred was a boy to include all manner of accessories for horse-drawn vehicles, the dominant mode of transportation at the time.

Alfred was apprenticed to his father in 1887, at the age of fifteen. Just a few years later, in 1892, a fire gutted the business, and at the age of fifty-one, Henry was attracted to retirement. The next year, he handed over control of the business to his son Alfred, who was a mere twenty-one years old.

In the few years that Alfred had been with the business, the world had made great headway in one of the most significant technological developments to affect mankind: the motorcar. It was here that Alfred Dunhill saw the future. (In fact, it is believed that Alfred became the proud owner of the third motorcar to appear on the open road in Great Britain.) So he immediately established a separate business, Dunhill's Motorities, to cater to the needs of this new form of transport.

Success was almost immediate; in the following few years the business expanded rapidly, and in 1902 included a shop that sold motoring accessories and clothing for ladies, gentlemen, and chauffeurs. On 21 November 1904, Alfred Dunhill filed patent application number 25,261 for a "windshield" pipe, granted the next year with the following specification:

> indispensable to the cyclist, the sportsman, the yachtsman, the automobilist, the billiard player . . . The shield, which is the feature of this pipe, prevents all inconvenience and danger of flying sparks or ash to the smoker and others when travelling on 'buses, tramcars, motor-cars, cycles, boats, etc. It ensures a cool, economical smoke, even in a gale. It overcomes the necessity of pressing down the tobacco after lighting, thus providing a free cool smoke, avoiding caking of tobacco, burning of fingers, or soiling of gloves.

Thus was born Alfred Dunhill's first pipe, and a new passion.

In 1907 he opened a tobacconist's shop in fashionable Duke Street, St. James's. London was a city of small shopkeepers, among them Alfred Dunhill. He went from strength to strength because of his high quality standards, attention to detail, and what was almost an obsession with the standard of service to the customer.

The shop was luxurious and refined, Alfred did the blending himself, and, like so many of his enterprises, it was an instant success. Pipe smokers were returning to the shop for more of their favourite and personal tobacco blends—"More of my mixture, please"—and so the *My Mixture* book was started. Over 36,700 individual blends, made up specially for customers, are now recorded in these volumes.

The shop also carried smokers' requisites—among them lighters, cigarette cases, cigarette holders, cigar cases, cutters, and tobacco pouches. He hung this sign in his window: "Sir—Can you speak of your pipe as a friend? If it is hot or fails to soothe, then consult Alfred Dunhill within, who will blend a tobacco suitable for your palate."

From the very beginning, the shop carried pipes, made elsewhere. But these fell far short of Alfred's conception of quality. At first the shop offered repair work, and then, in 1910, pipe workshops were opened in Duke Street, producing pipes that sold at double the prices of other makers. The White Spot was introduced a few years later, to guide smokers to the proper orientation of inserting mouthpieces to stems.

Alfred was joined in the business by his brother Herbert, who had an astute business acumen and looked after the financial side of the business, leaving Alfred to initiate and develop products—the perfect committee of two. The increasing success of the business was achieved more by word of mouth and recommendation than by commercial advertising. On the other hand, brilliance at marketing—and a certain degree of accident—played major roles, as in this ingenious campaign during the First World War:

Many of our customers were officers serving in the trenches of northern France. Whenever orders were received for a Dunhill pipe, Alfred sent off a box of twelve of them with a note suggesting that the others be offered to fellow officers. Invariably, all of them were sold rather than given away, and not only to the British but also to the Americans, Canadians, French, and Belgians. Such a box of pipes would also contain a roll of toilet tissue with a note that it might come in useful— for the box was sealed with a label reading "Castor Oil," without fail averting the prospect of pilferage.

By the end of the war, in 1918, the Dunhill pipe was known worldwide. Riding high on this rapid expansion of fame, in 1921 the firm was granted its first Royal Warrant, as Tobacconist to Edward, Prince of Wales.

It was, I suppose, only natural for my grandfather, who always became deeply involved with everything he did, to form a collection of pipes from around the world. In the early days these pipes were on display in the shop. This collection was extensively cataloged, and an archivist was employed to consolidate a comprehensive knowledge of pipes. Consequently, the company's expertise in the area grew, as did the firm's authority and reputation.

From the archives and the cataloged collection emerged an obvious, equally ambitious endeavour: *The Pipe Book*. First published simultaneously in London and New York in 1924, it was received with great enthusiasm by pipe smokers. It has rarely been out of print in the three quarters of a century since, and has always been regarded as a comprehensive—if somewhat eccentric—reference work, and, for collectors in particular, an invaluable guide.

That wonderful collection was, sadly, severely damaged in the Second World War, during the bombing raids on London. All the pipes, or what remained of them, were put into tea chests. It became my task to reestablish the collection by sorting, cleaning, and identifying each exhibit. I then had to mount the collection on display boards, by continent, in our newly rebuilt shop in Duke Street.

I joined the company in 1948, when the country was still suffering from postwar austerity and extensive shortages of raw materials. My first job, in the wholesale department, was thus made simple: we could supply only about half the merchandise that customers ordered, and consequently we encountered no "back order" problems.

The first departure from a totally smoking business started more by accident than by design. When we opened our shop in Paris in 1924, we were set back when the French tobacco monopoly refused to grant us a licence to sell tobacco products. In order to fill up the empty spaces, the manager decided to obtain gift items such as china, glass, and lacquerware. This idea worked so well in France that we decided to do the same in London and New York.

And so it was that Dunhill shops sold not just pipes, smokers' accessories, and general gift merchandise, but men's fashion accessories—ties, belts, slippers— and men's fragrances. For ladies, there were scarves, handbags, and jewellery, as well as writing instruments and watches.

In the 1970s we undertook an ambitious expansion in addition to our core business of smokers' products. We designed and developed a range of many of the products for men that we already had been retailing: menswear and fashion accessories, jewellery (including writing instruments and watches), fragrances, and leather goods. These are now standard to all Alfred Dunhill retail shops.

Alfred Dunhill Limited is to me a way of life and a family heritage, where goods of the highest quality are sold with impeccable service. *The Pipe Book* is an important legacy of that commitment—a study born of unlimited curiosity and the passion to serve the customer to the greatest degree possible, by knowing everything there is to know about the subject of pipes.

—Richard Dunhill
London, 1999

FOREWORD

CRITICS, *disarm! And ye, Antiquarians, Archæo-
logists, Ethnographers, Ethnologists,* et hoc genus
omne, *hold back in their leashes your quivering
Fountain-pens! For this is no learned Treatise,
but a simple Book, and written thus. Glancing
idly one day along the stout row of his Hobby-
horses, which were munching quietly in their stalls,
the Author spied a Newcomer, stabled there seemingly by Chance the night before. And casting his
leg across it, he rode his new Hobby afar into the
countryside and into Lands unknown. There did
he learn and see many Things, which afterwards he
wrote and drew in this Book. To the many, learned
and simple, who, as he rode, told the Author this and
that about his Hobby that he knew not before, he
hereby tenders his most grateful thanks.*

> " Give a man a pipe he can smoke,
> Give a man a book he can read,
> And his home is bright with a calm delight,
> Though the room be poor indeed."

ACKNOWLEDGMENT

FIGURES 9 and 10 are reproduced from the article by Henry Balfour, Esq., M.A., which appeared in *Man* for May, 1922, and are here reprinted by kind permission of the author and of the Royal Anthropological Society.

CONTENTS

THE PIPE BOOK

THE PIPE BOOK

CHAPTER I

WHY MEN SMOKE

THE story runs that when the tomb of the half-divine Callisto was removed to Paris, the immortal nymph wandered nightly through the gay quarters of the city seeking diversion. Chancing to enter the flat of a fashionable young Parisian, she lamented to him that in all the centuries that had elapsed since her former life mankind had devised not one new pleasure. Sighing assent, the young man idly handed her a cigarette, only to find, when he had shown her the use of the dainty tube of white and gold, that, quite inadvertently, he had given her what she craved, a new, and indeed exquisite, pleasure.

Smoking to-day is a pleasure almost as world-wide as music and dancing, yet only four hundred years ago it was quite unknown to the majority of the world's inhabitants. Nothing is more remarkable than the rapidity with which the new habit spread; it had only to be known to be immediately popular, and neither kingly nor priestly edicts, nor the violent tirades of self-styled moralists, could stem the rising tide of devotees to tobacco. The "Counterblaste to Tobacco" of our own King James I. has often been quoted; Shah Abbas the Great, a contemporary ruler of Persia, forbade it entirely; the Emperor Jahangir decreed that the smoker should have his lips slit, while in seventeenth-century Turkey any man found smoking had his nose pierced, and the pipe thrust through the hole. The result was that in the East smoking was for the time practised only in the privacy of the home, and we look in vain for mention of it in the narratives of early travellers in those parts.

Less than fifty years, however, after the death of King James, a French visitor to England has occasion to exclaim at the extraordinary prevalence there of smoking. "The supper being finished," he writes, "they set on the table half a dozen pipes, and a packet of tobacco for smoking, which is a general custom as well with women as with men, who think that without tobacco one cannot live in England, because, they say, it dissipates the evil humours of the brain. When the children went to school they carried in their satchel a pipe, which their mother took care to fill early in the morning, it serving them instead of breakfast; and at the accustomed hour everyone laid aside his book to fill his pipe, the master smoking with them and teaching them how to hold their pipe and draw in the tobacco, thus habituating them to it from their youth, believing it absolutely necessary for a man's health."

Perhaps we have solved the mystery of the widespread popularity of tobacco when we consider that it is the sole narcotic that can be employed repeatedly and even continuously without bringing in its train either physical discomfort or other ill effects. Nor is it merely soothing and consolatory; a thousand anecdotes speak of tobacco as enabling men to almost superhuman endurance. Thus, an English wanderer in the trackless forests of South America wrote: "As often before in time of trouble, we composed ourselves with a cigar. Blessed be the man who invented smoking, the soother and comforter of a troubled spirit, allayer of angry passions, a comfort under loss of breakfast, and to the roamer in desolate places, the solitary wayfarer through life, serving for wife, children, and friends." We have, too, the witness of the learned Jesuit, Joseph Acosta, who, writing in 1588 of the religious rites of ancient Mexico, describes an unction made of the ashes of " divers little venomous beastes," including " black and hairie worms," which were brazed in mortars with " much Tobacco or Petum (being an herb this nation useth much, to benum the flesh, that they may not feel their travail). . . . The Priests being slobbered with this ointment, lost all feare, putting on a Spirit of Crueltie. . . . This Petum did also serve to cure the sick, and for children ; and therefore all called it divine physicke." It was this aspect of " Tobacco as the Sovereigne Herbe "—the heal-all—that was prominent in Elizabethan days, and is satirized by Ben Jonson in his play " Every Man in his Humour" (1598), where he makes Captain Bobadil say : " Sir, believe me upon my relation, for what I tell you the world shall not reprove. I have been in the Indies where Tobacco grows, where neither myself, nor a dozen gentlemen more of myself, have received the taste of any other nutriment in the world, for the space of one and twenty weeks, but the fume of this simple only. Therefore it cannot be but it is most divine."

For the everyday smoke, however, what more is there to know of it than this, that it is, in its essence, the pipe of peace ? This is the idea which we find embodied in the folklore of simple peoples, as in the following Indian tale: " A Coyote had offered grievous insult to the head of a slain buffalo Bull. A living Bull pursued him to avenge his kinsman, but Manitou, the Great Spirit, taking pity on the Coyote's weakness, gave to him the first pipe and the first tobacco. To the angry Bull the pipe was offered as he flung himself at his enemy; and as he smoked the Coyote said to him: 'It will be thus in later times, when there will be many people. When they are angry with one another, they will smoke to make their hearts feel good.'"

The same truth is yet more delightfully expressed in a story taken down by Mr. Torday, the anthropologist, from the lips of an old Bushongo savage in a remote Congo village. The narrator was the Bilumbu, the mentor of his country's youth, and his home was Misumba in the province of N'Gong.

" Once upon a time, when Shamba Mkepe (whose memory be praised) was ruling the land of the Bushongo, there lived a man called Lusana Lumunbala. This man was of a restless humour; instead of staying quietly in his village, tilling his fields, herding his goats, chasing game and marrying many wives, he would roam all over the country from place to place. After a time he found

Bushongo too limited for his travels, though you all know how great it is this day, and in the days of Shamba it was by far greater; an irresistible longing for wider fields called him beyond its borders. Vainly did his elders try to dissuade him of his folly; like many young folk, he laughed at their earnest remonstrations, and could not resist the call of the unknown. Aye, aye, we all think that happiness dwells in the village where we are not.

" So one day he took his bow and arrows, and a bag full of food, and went off to the West. Years passed and no news from him reached his people—was it ten, twenty, thirty? Who knows? At any rate, so many that people lost count of them, and at last it was generally assumed that he had perished in his travels, and many were those who said: ' Serve him right, for being such a foolhardy man.'

" One evening a company of men were sitting round a fire in Misumba talking of the good old times. They were old: it is always the old men who revel in the past, while the young folk look forward to the mirages of the future. And neither the past nor the future are what they seem: the soft light of the moon shines on memories, while expectations are lit up by the glorious rays of the rising sun. Several of these men were of the age of Lusana Lumunbala, and had been initiated into the mysteries of the tribe in the same time as he; thus it came about that one of them mentioned his name, and all shook their grey heads over their age-brother's folly. As they were talking, a traveller covered with dust came from the road and sat down amongst them. Courtesy forbade them to question him, and he sat silently for a while. He scanned their faces and spoke at last: 'Is there not one among you, O men of Misumba, who knows me?' They looked at him and silently shook their heads. 'Not you, Bope Mikwete, nor yet you, Mikope?' But the two men knew him not. The stranger hung down his head wearily: 'The many years I have spent abroad must have changed me sadly if even the best friends of my youth have become strangers to me. Do not any of you remember Lusana Lumunbala the traveller?'

"All jumped up in amazement; they rushed up to him and touched him with their hands to make sure he was in the flesh, and not one of those ghosts who play pranks on innocent people; and when they were satisfied that he was still of this world there was great rejoicing among them. The news that the long-lost wanderer had come home again ran like wildfire through the village; men, women, and children thronged to see him, and brought abundance of presents to make him welcome. And they all sat down to a feast and did honour to Lusana Lumunbala.

" When the last goat was eaten, the last calabash emptied of palm-wine, and even the most intrepid tired of dancing, the elders invited the hero of the feast to sit down in their midst, and the Bami spoke thus to him: 'Now, Lusana Lumunbala, that we have shown you that you are welcome in your own home, be you healthy or sick, mean or powerful, rich or poor, tell us how you have fared in those foreign parts, and show us the curious things you have brought back from your travels. What treasures have you found? Let our eyes rejoice at the sight of the wonders, and maybe the riches, you have gathered on your enterprise.'

" The traveller searched in his bag and produced from it some dried leaves of tobacco and a little packet of seeds.

" 'Men of Bushongo,' he said solemnly, 'thank me from the bottom of your hearts, for I have brought you this.'

" The elders passed the leaves from hand to hand and shook their heads; one of them said sternly:

" ' Do you think, Lusana Lumunbala, that this is the time for jesting ? What good is this weed to us ?'

" ' I fear,' said another mockingly, 'that this man has not gained anything by his much-vaunted travels, and that the hardships which they have entailed have made him lose something. . . .' And he tapped his head significantly.

" Lusana Lumunbala smiled. ' I have not lost my reason, O elders of Misumba, for this weed of which I have brought you a sample is very precious indeed.'

" ' Is it good to eat ?'

" ' It is not.'

" ' Is it a remedy for some sickness ?'

" ' It soothes them all. Its smoke, when inhaled, is to the suffering soul as a mother's caress to an ailing child.'

" Saying so, he took a pipe out of his bag, filled it with a little tobacco, kindled it with some embers, and began to smoke, and as he did so his countenance beamed with happiness.

" The elders talked all at once : ' Surely our brother has become demented ; he now eateth fire and drinketh smoke.'

" But one of them, more courageous than the

others, asked him to let him try this wonderful weed, and taking the pipe inhaled a big whiff of smoke. He was taken with a violent fit of choking and fell to the ground gasping for breath. When he recovered he abused the traveller, and threatened him with his fist.

"'You are,' Lusana Lumunbala rebuked him, 'like an infant who chokes at the first mouthful of solid food his mother gives him, and yet, as he grows accustomed to it, becomes a brave companion at the trencher. You were too greedy. Little by little one filleth the basket, as the proverb says. You ought to have tried a little; if you do this you will soon enjoy the magic effect of the smoke as much as I do. For this weed, called Makaya, is man's greatest joy. I have learned its use in the land of Pende, whose inhabitants, the Tupende, have learned it from a strange people coming from beyond the salt water. O Makaya, Makaya, what wonders you can work!' And Lusana Lumunbala shut his eyes in ecstasy. 'As the fire will soften iron, so Makaya will soften the heart. If one day your brother has wronged you, and the blood rushes to your head in anger, and you reach out for your bow and arrows to slay him—take your pipe and smoke. Your ire will fly before its fragrance. You will say, "Surely I must not slay the son of my mother, him who is of my own blood. I will beat him with a big stick to teach him a lesson." But as you rise to fetch your cudgel, take your pipe and drink its smoke. And half-ways you will stop, and smile and say, " No, I cannot beat my brother, the companion of my youth. It is more becoming that I should scold him—lash him with bitter words instead of smiting him with a stick." And as you go to do so, smoke, smoke. And with every whiff your heart will become more charitable and forgiving, and as you come up to the trembling culprit you will throw your arms round his neck and say : " Brother, brother, let bygones be bygones ; come to my hut, and let us drink and eat together and be merry, and love each other." '

" And all of you know that Lusana Lumunbala spoke the truth ; whenever your heart rises in wrath or sinks in sorrow, drink the smoke of Makaya, and peace and happiness will reign in it again."

CHAPTER II

To make a pipe is by no means the affair of a moment or even of an hour : the bowl must be carved and hollowed, the stem bored and fitted, and the mouthpiece shaped smoothly to the lips. Hence the primitive savage who has lost or broken his pipe must often wait long before he can replace it, especially if the material that custom demands that he shall use is for the time being lacking. Many are the quaint expedients by which a make-shift smoke is obtained. The naturalist Brehm relates that on one occasion he entered the tent of a heathen Ostiak, and, as the surest way of winning a welcome, presented his host with a little tobacco. The man had no pipe ; but, fortunately, he had a bit of newspaper, the treasured gift of some Russian fur-trader. Twisting a piece firmly into a cornet, he bent up the wider end to form the bowl, and was soon sharing fragrant whiffs with his delighted wife and family. Curiously

12

enough, a pipe of similar pattern, but fashioned
from a *sal* leaf, is that in ordinary use among

certain Dra-
vidian hill-
tribes of Cen-
tral India, and

FIG. 1.—Pipe made from Twisted Leaf of Sal Tree,
Mirzapur.

as an occa-
sional make-
shift by the natives generally.   Such a pipe, now
in the Dunhill collection (collected and presented
by Mr. Henry Balfour), is shown in Fig. 1, and
below it (Fig. 2) is the somewhat similar makeshift of a Central African tribe.   These are the
Monbuttu, who live on the Upper Welle River,
a tributary of the Congo, of whom Schweinfurth,
the traveller, writes : " They smoke only Virginia
tobacco, and use pipes of a primitive but really
serviceable description made from the midrib of a
plantain leaf.   This is bored all through with a stick,
and near the extremity a small opening is
made, into which is inserted a plantain leaf,

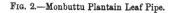

FIG. 2.—Monbuttu Plantain Leaf Pipe.

twisted up into a cornet and filled with tobacco.
This is changed as often as the pipe is lighted.

It is a contrivance that modifies the rankness
of the tobacco almost as perfectly as if it had
been inhaled from a Nargileh. The upper classes
occasionally smoke iron or copper pipes made
on the same principle, but always prefer inserted
cornets to a solid bowl."

The Eskimo of the remotest snow-wastes of
North America is naturally often hard put to it for
material. His clever makeshift is shown in Fig. 3.

FIG. 3.—Eskimo Makeshift Pipe of Willow.

This is merely a twig of dwarf willow, which has
been cut off together with its terminal node. The
latter has been scooped out to serve as a bowl,
while the stem has been split and the pith removed,
the two portions then being bound together again
with a raw-hide thong; the result is a very simple
affair, in strong contrast to the elaborate and
beautiful pipes in general use among these people,
which will be referred to later on. In tropical
countries where hollow rattans and bamboos
abound, a natural pipe is very quickly made. All
that is necessary is to cut off a shoot together with
the thickened part where it springs from the main
root or stem; the thickened portion is gouged out

for a bowl, and the pipe is ready. The sketch (Fig. 4) shows a pipe of this kind such as is

FIG. 4.—Coolie Pipe of Bamboo.[1]

commonly used by Chinese coolies. It is to be seen in Horniman's Museum. Two beautiful examples of the same type are to be seen in the Dunhill collection, and are figured in Plate II., but they have been lifted from the category of makeshifts, for some Siamese craftsman has skilfully mounted in metal the hollow that serves as a bowl. The ingenious way in which, in one case, lopped side-shoots have been retained as ornaments is worth noticing. Fig. 5 shows another graceful

FIG. 5.—Natural Bamboo Pipe from Szechwan.

little pipe of natural bamboo such as is smoked in Szechwan (Western China), and has thence been introduced into neighbouring Tibet. The pipe smoked by the bearded Ainus, that strange aboriginal people of North Japan, is of the same simple character, a mere hollowed stem from a

[1] The scale beside each pipe represents 1 inch.

birch or ash tree, cut so that part of the main stem
serves as a bowl (Fig. 6). A unique example in the
Dunhill collection has twin stems, a variant
suggested by the natural occurrence of twin shoots
(Plate II.).

The Kirghiz shepherd, lacking a pipe, makes a
clumsy affair from the knuckle-bone of a lamb that
has served the company for dinner. The marrow

FIG. 6.—Ainu Pipe of Natural Twig.

is scooped out, and a hole bored near the thicker
end of the bone serves as a bowl. Of a more gruesome
character is the bone-pipe in the possession of Mr.
Stanley Clark of the Victoria and Albert Museum
(Plate II.). This is made from the thigh-bone of a
little child, and the very small size of the hole cut
for the bowl suggests that it has been used for
opium. The pipe has evidently been in long use,
and has "coloured" as beautifully as a meerschaum.
Its exact place of origin is not known, but it
certainly came from China, and is attributed to one
of the savage tribes living in the southern hill-
country, who are held to be descended from the
aboriginal inhabitants of the whole region, a race

gradually ousted by the more civilized Chinese. Bloodshed is of so common occurrence among these people, that to obtain a human bone for a pipe would present no difficulty.

It is not only savage peoples who make use of natural objects as pipes: the sketch in Fig. 7 (made in Horniman's Museum) shows one of the seg- ments of a huge crab's claw, which, after the " meat " had been re- moved, was pierced at the narrow end and

FIG. 7.—Cornish Fisherman's Pipe of a Crab's Claw.

smoked as a pipe by a Cornish fisherman of Falmouth. Even this is not an innovation, for a seventeenth-century traveller records that the Red Indians of Nova Scotia made a similar use of a lobster's claw. Equally primitive is the English countryman's pipe, made from a natural elbow of tough gorse root, which is to be seen in the Dunhill collection (Fig. 8).

FIG. 8. — Country- man's Pipe of Gorse-root.

Among Red Indians a makeshift smoke is obtained by building a bowl on the ground from a clod of wet clay, and thrusting into the side of it a long hollow reed to serve as a stem. This is curiously reminiscent of the so-called "earth-smoking" with which travellers in Asia and Africa are familiar. Earth-smoking occurs in two widely separated areas of the Old World: one region including the grass-steppe and salt-steppe of Central and Western Asia, together with some remote valleys of Northern India abutting on the steppe, the other including the grass veld and Kalahari scrub-lands of South Africa. In both these areas easily worked wood is a great rarity, and the people are often of a wandering habit, and so make little use of stone or pottery. The population is scanty, so that villages, bazaars, or marts where a pipe might be purchased, are few and far between. To obtain a smoke when on the march, the native digs a little pit in the ground where he finds the soil suitable, and pushes a stick through the earth nearly horizontally until the point reaches the " bowl." The soil over the stick is pressed down until it is quite firm, and then the latter is withdrawn, leaving behind a hollow tube which serves as a "stem." To smoke such a pipe, the smoker must lie flat on the ground in an exceedingly uncomfortable position with his lips to the earth. Where, however, some natural cliff or terrace makes it possible, the pipe may be constructed on a level with the smoker's mouth, and this was actually done by Indian soldiers in the trenches during the Great War.

A slightly different form of earth - pipe is made by building up a little mound of damp clay and pressing it into the shape of a clumsy

FIG. 9.—An Earth-Smoker.   (After Henry Balfour.)

bowl; a few grass stems, rushes, or a thin stick are left embedded in one side of the lump, and are pulled out when it dries, thus forming a rudimentary stem.   Such a pipe has only about three

inches between bowl and mouthpiece, if such it may be called, and is even more awkward to smoke than the first type, as Fig. 9 clearly shows.   It is, however, an advance upon the " pit " earth-pipe, for

FIG. 10.—An Earth-Smoker.   (After Henry Balfour.)

once it is dry it can be detached from the ground, and so becomes a portable pipe.   Two fine speci-

mens made by South African Hottentots are to be
seen in the Dunhill collection (Plate III.), one
merely of the "lump" type, while the other is
almost worthy of the name of "pipe." A number
of specimens can be seen in the Pitt Rivers
Museum at Oxford, the Curator, Mr. Henry
Balfour, being an authority on the subject of

earth - smoking.
He suggests that
the method lin-
gers on in Africa
in spite of the
abundant "trade"
pipes, because it

FIG. 11.—Kashmir Pipe of Unbaked Clay.

provides a means of surreptitious hemp-smoking,
a dangerous practice which is forbidden. The
pipe of unbaked clay from Kashmir, in the North-
West of India (Fig. 11), though better shaped than
the crude earth-pipe is probably a derivative of
such a pipe.

The earth-pipe, even when portable, cannot be
held between the teeth ; the mouth is merely
pressed against an orifice. The question suggests
itself, Are we not here on the track of the evolution
of pipes and pipe-smoking ? Is not the practice a
development of the inhalation of narcotic smoke

in early times from an open fire ? In an oft-quoted passage, Herodotus writes as follows of a certain Scythian tribe (a people native to the very land where earth-smoking is practised to-day) : " They have also a tree which bears the strangest produce. When they are met together in companies they throw some of it upon the fire round which they are sitting, and presently, by the mere smell of the fumes which it gives out in burning, they grow drunk, as the Greeks do with wine. More of the fruit is then thrown on the fire, and, their drunkenness increasing, they often jump up and begin to dance and sing. Such is the account which I have heard of this people." The fruit referred to is supposed to have been hemp, and it would be a natural thing for an individual to burn a few grains for himself over a handful of embers in a little pit, holding his face above the fire to inhale the smoke. Then to some inventive mind occurred the more economical and effective process of drawing the smoke into the lungs through a tube or orifice in the side of the fire, and thus the earth-pipe came into being.

The archaic or primitive form of a custom is often preserved (even after novelties have come into general use) in the method by which it is performed on ceremonial occasions, for under such circumstances the ancient ritual is followed out to the letter. If this is the case, then a practice of the Indians of Darien suggests that in America also individual smoking is a development of the inhalation of smoke rising into the air, which was quite possibly done when the priest " censed " the worshippers.

The practice referred to is described in Wafer's " Travels," dated 1681. " These Indians," he says, " have tobacco among them. When it is dried and cured they strip it from the stalks, and laying two or three leaves upon one another, they roll up all together sideways into a long roll, yet leaving a little hollow. Round this they roll other leaves one after another, in the same manner, but close and hard, till the roll be as big as one's wrist, and two or three feet in length. Their way of smoking when in company together is this : a boy lights one end of the roll, burning it to a coal, wetting the part next to it to keep it from wasting too fast. The other end he puts into his mouth, and blows the smoak of the roll into the face of every one of the company or council, though there be two or three hundred of them. Then they, sitting in their usual posture, make, with their hands held hollow together, a kind of funnel round their mouths and noses. Into this they receive the smoak as it blows upon them, snuffing it up greedily and strongly, as long as ever they are able to hold their breath ; and seeming to bless themselves, as it were, with the refreshment it gives them."

The practice of an individual " smoking over " other persons and objects for religious purposes was widespread in North America, and will be referred to again

FIG. 12.—Maya Priest smoking Tube-Pipe.

later. In this connection the famous bas-relief of a Maya priest engaged in the act of ceremonial smoking is of peculiar interest. An outline sketch of this piece of sculpture (of which a cast is now to be seen in the British Museum) is reproduced in Fig. 12. The pipe is a simple tube, tapering towards the mouthpiece (such tube-pipes are discussed in detail in the following chapter), and to judge from a comparison with the smoker's hands,

is 8 or 9 inches long. The bas-relief is carved on a large stone slab which formed one of a pair set in the wall on either side of the Temple of the Cross at Palenque, a site in the modern state of Chiapas in the extreme south of Mexico. The date of this temple is about A.D. 114,

FIG. 13.—Maya God Chac with Tube-Pipe.

but the custom of making the smoke offering, as shown on the slab, must have already been many hundreds of years old. Chac, the Maya god of fertility, is sometimes represented, as shown in Fig. 13, carrying a similar tube-pipe; while smoking figures are not infrequent in the picture writings that have been discovered — *e.g.*, the seated man in Fig. 14. The culture of the Mayas, which mysteriously dis-appeared long before the conquest

FIG. 14.—Maya Man Smoking Tube-Pipe.

of Mexico, was the inspiration of that of their northern neighbours the Toltecs, and it was from the Toltecs that the Aztec civilization was in its turn derived; thus the ancient Mexican or Aztec smoking customs, first observed by the Spaniards and presently to be described, can be traced back to this forgotten people, the Mayas of Central America.

Nor are we justified in looking upon the Mayas as the true originators of the use of tobacco. They, in their turn, derived their culture from an alien source—namely, from those brown-skinned men, sun-worshippers and builders of great stone monuments, who filtered eastwards half round the world from their home on the Mediterranean Sea during the fifteen thousand years that preceded the birth of Christ. Some of their direct descendants are to be found in the East Indies to this day, and, according to Dr. Kruyt, the Dutch anthropologist, it is almost certain that these people made use of tobacco, probably in connection with their worship, more than two thousand years ago; they only gave it up when newcomers from Asia, ancestors perhaps of the Malays, overran their islands, and introduced the custom of betel-chewing.

The recent observations made by Mr. Austen, a Government official in Papua, upon the little-known tribes of the upper basin of the Fly River, are consistent with Dr. Kruyt's suggestions. These people do not use the big-stemmed inhaling pipes common to the coastal peoples, but merely a straight or slightly bent piece of bamboo, from 9 to 18 inches long and $\frac{3}{4}$ inch in diameter (Fig. 15). The tobacco, which is known as *a-up*,

FIG. 15.—Bamboo Tube-Pipe from Inner Papua.

and not by any corruption of its European name as in most localities, is rolled in a leaf and inserted in the end of bamboo, as though the latter were a cigarette-holder. This may be the archaic pipe form, which, as a number of facts suggest, was always the simple tube. To prevent the ash being drawn into the mouth, a teased-out sago-leaf is used as a plug, a device also employed in the big bamboo pipe of Borneo. It may be, of course, that the simple bamboo tube (Benget) is actually a derivative from the normal introduced form, or, rather, is a crude substitute for it, but the facts open up a fresh field for speculation and research.

That tobacco, as a species of incense, had a sacred character among its earliest users, we are reminded again and again. Thus, in the well-known passage from Hariot's account of Sir Walter Ralegh's first colony in Virginia the religious use of tobacco by the Red Indians to make a "sweet savour" for the Unseen Powers is referred to. "This Up-po-woc is of so precious distinction amongst them, that they think their gods are marvellously delighted therewith, whereupon sometimes they make hallowed fires and cast some of the powder therein for sacrifice."

From the makeshift pipe it is natural to turn to makeshift tobaccos, for since (owing to climatic conditions) the herb itself is by no means of world-wide cultivation, many substitutes for the weed have from time to time been employed. Thus the Red Indians of the colder parts of America smoked dried leaves of the sumach, the inner bark of the red willow, and the leaves and bark of several other shrubs. In Tibet wild rhubarb-root is used as an adulterant, and in Britain coltsfoot, yarrow, and moss have served the same purpose, the henbane or coltsfoot being sometimes known as English tobacco. The coltsfoot is also used in China. Yet another substitute is suggested in a humorous English dialogue dated 1599. "Have you a pipe of good tobacco?" the guest inquires. "There's none in the house, sir." "Then dry a dock leaf."

That the Congo pygmies, among the most timid and childlike of the human race, rarely coming into contact with other men, should have to fall back on makeshifts we can well imagine, and of them we read: "A three-foot length of bamboo cane is used as a pipe, with charcoal and smouldering leaves in place of tobacco."

How a makeshift of a most unpleasant character was forced upon an unwilling circle of smokers we read in the chronicles of that same Shah Abbas the Great who tried without avail to put down smoking in his dominions. He therefore summoned his courtiers to his presence, providing them with pipes filled with a mixture which he himself had caused to be prepared. At intervals he inquired of his guests as to their enjoyment, praising the new custom in no measured terms, and they answered him as courtesy to their sovereign demanded. But Shah Abbas smiled cynically as he listened to their flowery compliments, for the bowl of each pipe was filled with horses' dung!

CHAPTER III

IT has been suggested in the last chapter that the roughly hollowed lump of clay with its side orifice, which provides a makeshift pipe for the poorer folk in certain parts of South Africa and Asia, marks a step in the evolution of pipe-smoking, as distinguished from the inhalation of smoke from an incense burner or from an open fire. It appears quite possible also that in some parts of America the pipe was a development of the mere roll of leaves or primitive cigar. In the West Indies and Central America, at the time of their discovery, pipes were not known, and tobacco was taken either in a cigar or as snuff. Las Casas, the chronicler of Columbus, reports that the Indians of Hispaniola (visited 1492) had always " a fire-brand in their hand, and certain herbs for smoking. These were dry, and placed in a dry leaf, after the manner of those paper tubes which boys in Spain use at Whitsuntide." In many parts of the

29

southern United States tobacco was rolled up into a maize leaf for smoking, and it is an obvious and natural transition from such practices to insert the rolled-up tobacco into a tube of some sort, when a cooler and more complete smoke is possible.   Such

Fig. 16.—Maya Smoker in Recumbent Position.

was the pipe of the Maya priest already described, and also of the Aztecs of ancient Mexico, who were reported by the early Spanish historians to use tubes of tortoiseshell, silver, wood or reed, for their customary after-dinner smoke, and since the literal meaning both of the Spanish word *cañutos* (pipe) and of the English word " pipe " is simply a " hollow tube," it may be inferred that the smoking apparatus to which the name was first given was of that simple character, the word afterwards being extended to all types of pipes. To call these first tubular pipes cigar-holders, although they resemble the latter in pattern, would be incorrect, for the tobacco leaf was merely loosely rolled, for insertion, or was cut up and mixed with other substances. The obvious defect of the tube-pipe is that the tobacco is likely to fall out, and this difficulty was overcome by pressing in a little pebble, or by adopting a recumbent posture, as shown by the figure of the Maya smoker (Fig. 16). A plug of grass inserted before filling the pipe prevents the ash from falling into the mouth.

Where the tube was made in pottery, an accidental distortion in firing might produce such noticeable improvement that in future a bent tube is deliberately made. From the bent-up portion the different forms of bowl have been developed, while

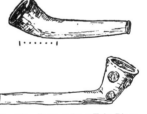

Fig. 17.—Pottery Bent-Tube Pipes.

the straight portion is modified into stem and mouthpiece. The two Red Indian specimens in pottery shown in Fig. 17 are examples of a form which seems to be intermediate between the

tube-pipe and the pipe with a bowl. The specimen in Fig. 18 is of finely grained syenite, and is
highly polished; it came from a burial mound in
Sullivan County, Tennessee. Over wide areas,
however, no transition from the straight
form was made, and especially in the
mountain and coast areas of North
America tube-pipes
were the rule among
the Indians, while
in the east of the
country, though

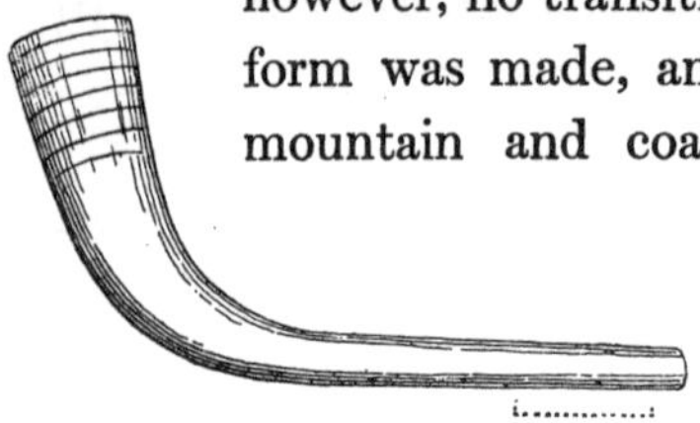

FIG. 18.—Bent-Tube Pipe of Syenite.

less common, they were not unknown.

As regards materials, a reed or cane as used in
Mexico affords a natural tube, but is not very
durable; still more fragile is the tube rolled from
birch-bark, a material put to this, among a hundred
other uses, by the Forest
Indians of Nova Scotia
and Newfoundland. A
bone makes a more satis-
factory pipe, and has been
used in the examples
shown in Fig. 19; the

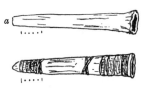

FIG. 19.—Two Red Indian Tube-
Pipes of Bone.

Comanche pipe (Fig. 19, *b*) is bound with raw hide.
Wood is frequently used, *e.g.*, by the Hupa

Indians (Fig. 20), but in primitive times stone
of some easily worked variety, frequently sand-
stone or steatite (soap-
stone, pot-stone), was
most commonly em-
ployed, or sometimes
serpentine (Fig. 21),
which takes on a fine
polish.

FIG. 20.—Wooden Tube Pipe of Hupa
Indians.

Pottery was the material most in favour
with the Pueblo Indians of New Mexico and

FIG. 21.—Serpentine Tube Pipe, California.

Arizona (Fig. 22). These people were sedentary
in their habits, and hence pottery-making among
them had reached a high level of development,

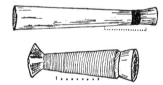

FIG. 22.—Pottery Tube Pipes,
Pueblo Indians.

whereas among wander-
ing, hunting tribes, to
which a majority of
Indians belonged, pot-
tery objects, being fra-
gile, were but little
used, and most domestic
articles were of stone, bone, or wood.

At the British Museum, stone tubes which have

all the appearance of tobacco pipes are to be seen among the objects taken from prehistoric grave

FIG. 23.—Tube from Prehistoric Grave, California.

sites in California (Figs. 23 and 24), but it is impossible to assign any definite date to the inception

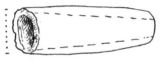

FIG. 24.—Stone and Bone Tubes from Prehistoric Grave, California.

of smoking. Interesting speculations are aroused, however, by the discovery of a stone tube bearing a close resemblance to Indian stone pipes in a Cretan Bronze Age site at Klaudia, Cyprus. A sketch and a cross-section are shown in Fig. 25, and the inference that we have here some sort of implement for smoking is irresistible; but, of course, no direct evidence can be

FIG. 25.—Stone Tube from Cretan Site in Cyprus.

forthcoming, as Cretan written records have not been deciphered. The period of the site is about

2000 B.C., when the Cretan civilization was at the height of its splendour; and although tobacco was of course unknown to these people, the inhalation of exhilarating or intoxicating herbs might well have been practised. That other kinds of smoking preceded that of tobacco is shown by the mention in Bana's "Kadambari," an Indian work of the seventh century A.D., that in India "cigars of scents were made and smoked." Indeed, the "Natural History" of Pliny contains several references to medicinal inhalation of various fumes passed through a funnel or reed; hence to identify stone and bone tubes of suitable dimensions as having been used for this purpose is by no means extravagant. A possible example is the bone tube in Fig. 26 a; this was found in Donkerbottom Cave, Yorkshire, and dates from the Roman occupation of Britain. It resembles so closely the Bushman woman's bone pipe

FIG. 26.—a, Romano-British Bone Tube; b, Bone Tube Pipe of Bushman Woman.

(Fig. 26 b) that it is very tempting to speculate upon its probable use for a similar purpose.

It is a curious fact that, apart from North and South America, the principal area in which the

straight or tube pipe is found is South-West
Africa, where it is smoked by the Bushmen and
Hottentots, and especially by the women of these
races. This further suggests that the tube is one
of the more archaic pipe forms, for it is very
commonly the case that a clumsy or old-fashioned
type of implement remains in use among women,
side by side with an improved or
newly invented form of the same
implement in use among men: the
knives of the Australian aborigines
afford an example.
The Hottentot men
either smoke "trade"
pipes or imitate them

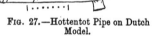

FIG. 27.—Hottentot Pipe on Dutch
Model.

in native materials: the illustration (Fig. 27)
shows an imitation of a Dutch clay in serpentine.
The serpentine pipe, used by a Bushman woman,
and shown in Fig. 28, should be compared with

FIG. 28.—Serpentine Pipe of Bushman
Woman.

the Red Indian ex-
ample, in the same
material, in Fig. 21.
The existence of
earth-smoking, as already described, and the use
of the tube pipe in Africa are but part of a series
of facts that have given rise to a theory that the

custom as found in that Continent was not brought over from America ; indeed, Professor Leo Weiner goes so far as to say that the reverse is the case, and that Africa gave tobacco to America less than a century before Columbus. This interesting speculation will be referred to again in connection with certain peculiar African pipes.

What is usually accepted as the earliest written description of a tobacco-pipe is that by Oviedo in his " History of the Indies," written in 1535. The implement he refers to is a two-pronged or Y-shaped tube. The two prongs were apparently held to the nostrils, and the use of the tube was to inhale tobacco or other smoke from a fire or censer, so that while it can hardly be termed a pipe, its use confirms the supposition that smoking was a development of inhalation.

Following closely in point of time upon Oviedo's description is that found in the narrative of Jacques Cartier's exploration of the St. Lawrence estuary, concluded in 1536. " They [i.e., the Indians] have likewise a certain herb of which they lay up store every summer, having first dried it in the sun. This is only used by the men, who always carry some of this dried herb in a small skin bag hanging from their necks, in which they also carry a hollow

piece of stone or wood like a pipe [*i.e.*, like the
musical instrument which that word denotes].
When they use this herb, they bruise it into a
powder, which they put into one end of the before
mentioned cornets or pipes, and lay a small piece
of live coal upon it, after which they suck so long
at the other end that they fill their bodies full of
smoke, till it comes out of their mouths and nostrils,
as if from the chimney of a fireplace.   They allege
that this practice keeps them warm and is con-
ducive to health.   We have tried to use this
smoke, but on putting it to our mouths, it seemed
as hot as pepper."

In English literature, according to the "New
English Dictionary," the word "pipe" in the
sense of "tobacco pipe" appears for the first
time in 1594, but in 1564 John Sparke, who
accompanied John Hawkins on his voyage to the
Indies and Florida, described a pipe without being
able to put a name to it.   "The Floridians," he
writes, "have a kinde of herbe dried, who
with a cane and an earthen cup in the end,
with fire, and the dried herbs put together, doe
sucke throw the cane the smoke thereof, which
smoke satisfieth their hunger, and therewith
they have four or five days without meate or

drinke, and this all the Frenchmen used for this purpose."

What appears to be the earliest reference to tobacco-smoking in Europe is to be found in a botanical work, by Doctors Pena and Lobel, printed in London in 1570, and dedicated to Queen Elizabeth. In the section headed *Indorum sana Sancta, vive Nicotiana Gallorum*, the learned authors discuss the fact that tobacco has by some been identified with henbane, owing to the fact that they have seen persons intoxicated with its smoke (hence the inhalation of henbane fumes must have been known). The passage con-

tinues: "You may see many sailors, and all those who come back from America, carrying little funnels (*pusilla infundibula*) made from a palm leaf or a reed, in the extreme end of which they insert the rolled and powdered dried leaves of this plant." The authors had themselves smoked the weed, and found that its effects differed from those of henbane. The interest of this passage is increased

FIG. 29.—Woodcut of Smoker, 1570.

by the woodcut annexed to it (re-sketched in Fig. 29), which shows a smoker making use of a cornet-shaped tube pipe, his head being thrown right back, and the pipe being unsupported by the hands. The legend runs: "Nicotiana inserta infundibulo ex quo hauriunt fumii Indi et naucleri." The two doctors apparently confirmed the view that tobacco was valuable in medicine: "Istius vero sanctæ herbæ vocatæ jam ubique increbuit fama," and no doubt this important pronouncement prepared the way for the spread of smoking from the seaports to the country at large.

Young Walter Ralegh (as he then was) had been the companion of sailors and adventurers, including his step-brother, Humphrey Gilbert, during his boyhood in Devon, and as a young man in his teens had served as a volunteer with the French Huguenots, from whose ranks were drawn the earliest colonists and explorers of Florida, referred to by John Sparke as smokers. Thus he had every opportunity to observe and imitate the practice of smoking, and coming up to London soon after the publication of Lobel's book, he was probably the first young man about town to set the fashion.

Only three years later (1573) the following notice appears in Harrison's "Chronology": "In these daies the taking in of the smoke of the Indian herbe

called Tabaco, by an instrument formed like a little
ladell, whereby it passeth from the mouth into the
hed and stomach, is gretlie taken up and used in
England." Both this and John Sparke's description refer obviously to a pipe with a small bowl,
for straight tube pipes were never made regularly
in Europe, although, according to the Spanish

physician Monardes,
who published a medi-
cal work in 1565, cane
and reed tubes were
brought to his country
from New Spain, and

Fig. 30.—The Dunhill "Onion" Tube
Pipe.

inhalation through them was recommended for
asthma. The tube pattern is, however, occasion-

Fig. 31.—*a*, Tube Pipe from Afghanistan ; *b*, Tube Pipe from Japan.

ally copied by pipe-makers of to-day to suit
individual needs or caprices (*e.g.*, the Dunhill
"onion," Fig. 30), and it is probable that the two
elaborate straight pipes in the illustration (Fig. 31),

of which one comes from Afghanistan and the other from Japan, have been "made to order." Tubular pipes are used in Paraguay, and also in such widely separated areas as the Aurès Mountains (North Africa) and the Philippines, but they are subsidiary to other patterns in these areas, and their significance will be discussed in its proper place in later chapters.

CHAPTER IV

WHEREVER the belief in a future life is strong among simple people, the custom prevails of burying with the dead such of their possessions as they may require in the Land of Spirits. Such was the custom among the Red Indians of North America, and since to this people the pipe was a sacred as well as a dear possession, many pipes of antique pattern have been recovered from grave sites. The Indians of the great Algonquin race, which included the Chippewa, Delaware, and Shawnee tribes, were accustomed to build over the graves of their dead earth-mounds, closely resembling the tumuli which are a familiar feature in our English chalk hills, and the systematic excavation of these mounds has thrown much light on early Indian arts and crafts, among which pipe-making held a conspicuous place. The Muskogee Indians, although of quite a different race to the Algonquins, were also mound builders,

their country being the area now comprising the
Gulf States, to the north of the Gulf of Mexico.
The home country of the Algonquins was originally
near the Great Lakes, but they were gradually
driven southwards down the Ohio and Mississippi
valleys by the pressure of more northerly tribes,
until finally some of them were neighbours of the
Muskogee. The consequence is that the older
Algonquin mounds are found in the north—
e.g., in Ohio, where is the famous Mound City—
and the newer ones are further south, and it is
in the Ohio mounds that the most interesting
pipes occur. The old idea that these great burial
mounds were the monuments of some civilized
non-Indian race (perhaps the ancestors of the
ancient Mexicans) has been abundantly disproved.
They are the work of the Indians who were met
with on the discovery of America, and in
particular of the tribes who practised systematic
agriculture, which was favoured by the soil and
climate, one of the more important of the crops
being tobacco. The religious observances of the
Algonquins included totem worship ; that is to
say, each clan or subdivision of a tribe held some
particular animal to be sacred to it, and in some
way to represent the clan : many legends made

the totem the ancestor of the clan and it served the
members as a tribal emblem, while it could not
be slain or hunted by them.   The Indian craftsman
lavished the utmost care on the carving of his
totem animal, and it is because such figures,
beautifully sculptured in stone, are characteristic of
many mound pipes, that these possess so great an
interest and value.

The characteristic shape of the unornamented
grave mound pipe is seen in Fig. 32, and it will

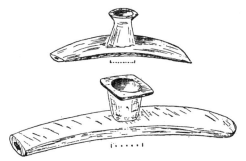

FIG. 32.—Two Typical Mound Pipes.

be noticed at once that it has no resemblance to
any type of pipe met with elsewhere.   The bowl
is mounted on a riband-like base, which is curved
slightly downwards, and projects equally in either
direction, the front portion serving for the smoker
to hold the pipe, while the back portion is both

stem and mouthpiece. The evolution of such a pipe-form can only be conjectured, but certain finds of a peculiar character in the grave mounds make it reasonable to suppose that it was developed, like the more normal type, from the simple tube pattern. In Figs. 33 and 34 two tubes taken from a mound

FIG. 33.—Tubular Mound Pipe and Section.

are shown, the longer being of slate, the shorter of limestone. The cleavage panes of the slate have allowed the maker to carve and polish the wing-like extension of the mouthpiece of the first tube, but in both cases the character of the tapering bore, shown in the section, points to the use of the tubes as pipes. Alter-

FIG. 34.—Tubular Mound Pipe of Limestone.

native suggestions are that they were musical instruments, or that they were used by the medicineman to suck out disease, as in the case of the bone tube sketched in Fig. 35. As a matter of fact, although the latter explanation may be correct, it in no way contradicts the theory that the tubes were smoking implements, for we find an early traveller describing the twofold use of such a tube among the Indians of California. He writes as follows : "One mode [of healing disease] was very

Fig. 35.—Tube for sucking out Disease.

remarkable, and the good effect it sometimes produced heightened the reputation of the medicine-man advising it. They applied to the suffering part of the patient's body the chacuaco, a tube formed of very hard, black stone ; and through this they sometimes sucked and sometimes blew, but both as hard as they were able, supposing that the disease was either exhaled or dispersed. Sometimes the tube was filled with cinaram or wild tobacco lighted, and here they either sucked in or blew down the smoke, according to the medicine-man's directions ; and this powerful caustic sometimes, without any other remedy, has been known entirely to remove the disorder." It is highly probable, then, that the tubes from the mounds were thus used. Since, moreover, medicine and religion are not separable in the minds of primitive people, this explains also the sacred character which pipe-

smoking, as a species of magic, was held to possess
by the Indians.

The first stage in the transformation of these
tube pipes is shown in Fig. 36, where, as will be
seen, the totem object of the clan, in this case an

owl, is carved in the
round on one side
of the tube. This
particular tube is a
very large one, mea-
suring ten inches in

FIG. 36.—Great Tube Pipe with Owl Totem.

length, and being of stone, is consequently very
heavy, but such an exaggeration of size beyond the
limits of convenience is a feature of ceremonial
pipes. Once the totem figure appeared on the
tube pipe, it would be a natural modification, in
the case of those not used for healing purposes, to
make the figure serve
as bowl, the tube
being flattened and
curved to serve as a
base, as shown in

FIG. 37.—Mound Pipe with Beaver Totem.

Fig. 37. The totem figure on the pipe in the illustration is the beaver, which is carved so as to face
the smoker, as in every pipe of this type. The
sketch gives only a slight idea of the lifelike and

spirited character of the carving, and it was the beauty of such sculptured figures that led so many investigators to doubt their Indian authorship. Certainly they are far superior to the work of the same character executed by Indians since the Discovery, but in the history of every nation we may observe such cycles of growth and decay in the sphere of the plastic arts, as a study of Egyptian and Greek sculptures and of European paintings will immediately reveal. The mound-builders were the

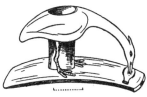

FIG. 38.—Mound Pipe with Heron Totem.

"Old Masters" of the Indian tribes. In Fig. 38 a second example of a totem pipe is given; in this case the animal is a tufted heron, in the act of striking a fish. The "pigeon" pipe (Tennessee) in Fig. 39, again very cumbersome, is intermediate in type between the tube-pipe and that with a flat base. A fact

FIG. 39.—Great Pipe of Pigeon Design.

which so far remains mysterious is that there are several examples of pipes upon which the craftsman has accurately depicted an animal which it seems impossible that he could have known. There is, for instance, the famous "elephant" pipe, showing an animal with a trunk, yet there are no elephants at all in the New World: and even should it be meant for the long-snouted tapir, the latter belongs only to Central and South America, and is not to be found within a thousand miles of Ohio. There are also many pipes showing unmistakably the manitee, or sea-cow, which haunts tropical rivers and shores, but which is never found further north than Florida. The hypothesis is sometimes put forward that such carvings date back to a time when the climate and animals of North America differed from those of to-day, but there is no evidence that the mounds belong to such remote periods, and it is simpler to suppose that the sculptor visited distant regions or derived his knowledge from some traveller.

FIG. 40.—Mound Pipe with Female Head.

In place of the totem figure, the bowl of the mound pipe is often a human head, or a human figure, and in Fig. 40 is given a sketch of the most famous example of this class; the strong, clean modelling of this female head is in some ways reminiscent of the best examples of Ancient Egyptian sculpture, and is far above the level of merely savage art.

FIG. 41.—Great Pipe with Kneeling Figure.

The kneeling Indian in Fig. 41 shows a decided falling off in fidelity to nature, and the conventionalized modelling of the face is very similar to that on the famous Ralegh pipe in the Dunhill collection, which is attributed to the Indians of Virginia. The "kneeling Indian" pipe has an orifice in the buttocks for

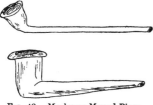

FIG. 42.—Muskogee Mound Pipes.

the insertion of a stem, and its dimensions show it to be one of the "great pipes" made for special ceremonial use, of which the tube with the owl totem is also an example.

The pipes taken from the burial mounds of the

Muskogees, who inhabited the south-east of the United States, were of patterns such as that in Fig. 42—*i.e.*, of the type we suppose to have evolved from the bent-up tube pipe. It was

from the Indians of this region that most Europeans learnt the art of pipe-smoking, and hence these are the prototype of European pipes to be referred to later. The two specimens in Figs. 43 and 44 give a further ex-

FIG. 43.—Indian Pipe with Human Figure.

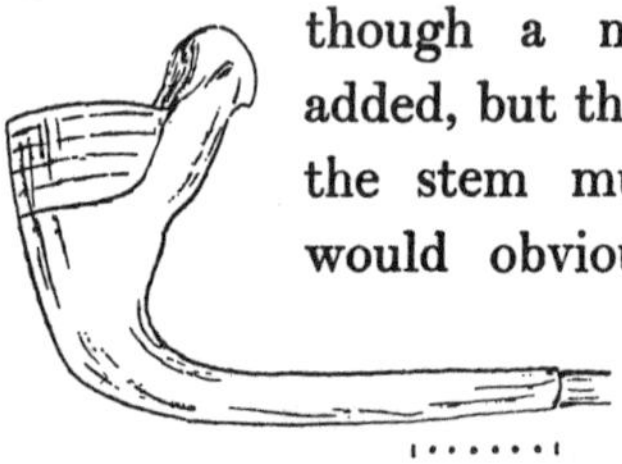

ample of a spirited piece of carving, and a debased or degenerate piece on similar lines. In the older pipes, bowl and stem are made all in one piece,

though a mouthpiece was often added, but the frequency with which the stem must have been broken would obviously have necessitated the addition of a make-shift stem, and later the manufacture of a separate bowl designed

FIG. 44.—Indian Pipe with Degenerate Carving.

for the insertion of a wooden stem, as in Fig. 45.

The pipes shown in Figs. 46 and 47, taken from mounds in Ohio and West Virginia, have charac-

teristics intermediate between the simple mound
pipe of Fig. 56 and the Muskogee pipe: the bowl

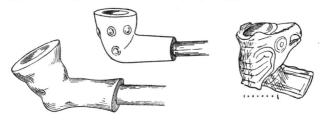

FIG. 45.—Three Mound Pipes for use with Stem.

is gradually moved from its central position though
remaining at right angles to the stem, and the flat

FIG. 46.—Mound Pipe of Transitional Character.

stem-base gradually approximates to the ordinary
tube stem.

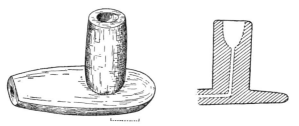

FIG. 47.—Large Mound Pipe of Transitional Character.

CHAPTER V

INDIAN PIPES AND PIPE MYSTERIES

THE most arresting and most frequently discussed aspect of pipe-smoking among the Red Indians was its symbolic use in the council circle, and between nations, when the question of peace or war hung in the balance.

The ascent and vanishing of smoke have always appeared charged with mystery to the untutored mind, and among the Indians of the Plains the pipe was regarded as the instrument by which the breath of man ascended to God through the fragrant smoke, carrying with it the prayer or aspiration of the smoker. The act partook also of the nature of an oath, and so was used to seal an agreement, whether public or private. The ceremonials of the Omaha tribe, which have been carefully studied by the American Bureau of Ethnology, may be taken as typical of those of the Plains Indians in general—that is to say, of the indians who lived by buffalo hunting, and whose

PLATE I

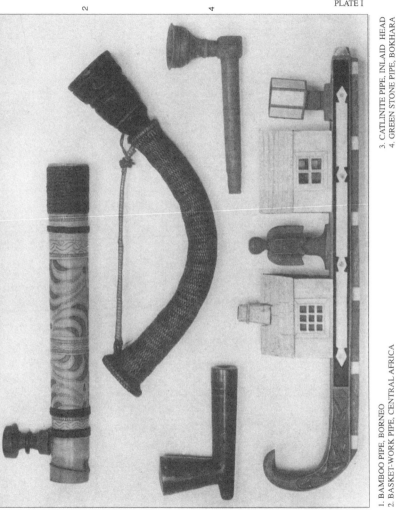

1. BAMBOO PIPE, BORNEO
2. BASKET-WORK PIPE, CENTRAL AFRICA
3. CATLINITE PIPE, INLAID HEAD
4. GREEN STONE PIPE, BOKHARA
5. RED INDIAN PIPE, NORTH-WEST COAST *(in the British Museum)*

PLATE II

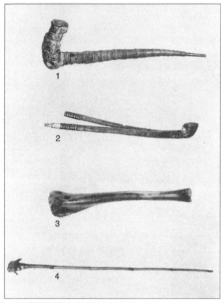

1 and 4. PIPES OF NATURAL BAMBOO
2. AINU PIPE WITH TWIN STEMS
3. CHINESE PIPE OF HUMAN BONE

PLATE III

HOTTENTOT EARTH PIPES

PLATE IV

1. CHIPPEWA PIPE WITH SNAKE STEM
2. CHIPPEWA PIPE WITH TOTEM
3. SIOUX PIPE OF STEATITE

4. TONGA CLUB PIPE
5. TOMAHAWK PIPE
6. A CHIPPEWA PIPE

PLATE V

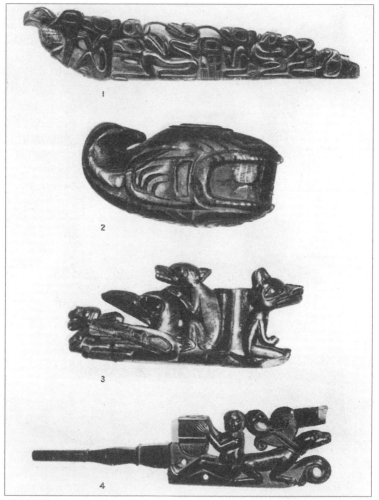

1. SLATE PIPE OF N. AMERICA
2. KILLER WHALE PIPE

3. SLATE PIPE
4. SLATE PIPE SHOWING
EUROPEAN INFLUENCE

PLATE VI

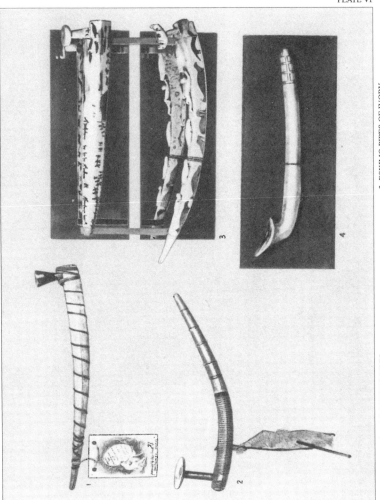

1 and 2. ESKIMO PIPES

3. ESKIMO PIPES OF IVORY
4. PIPE OF MAMMOTH IVORY

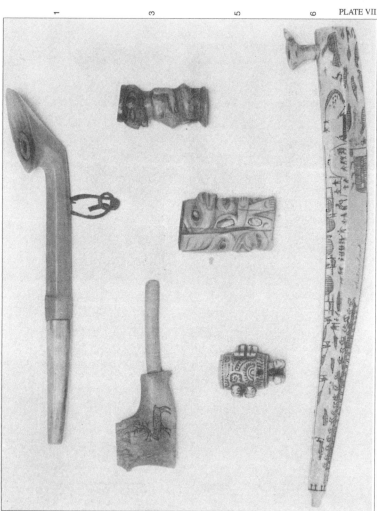

PLATE VII

1. MAMMOTH IVORY PIPE, NORTH SIBERIA
2. HORN AND BONE PIPE, LAPLAND
3. CENTRAL AFRICAN PIPE OF IVORY
4. CACHALOT TOOTH PIPE, MARQUESAS
5. RED INDIAN PIPE OF WALRUS IVORY (*in the British Museum*)
6. WESTERN ESKIMO PIPE OF WALRUS IVORY

PLATE IX

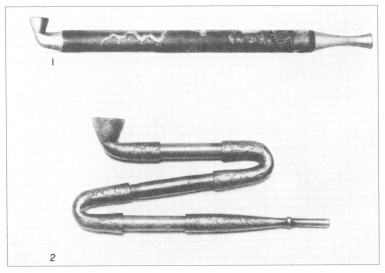

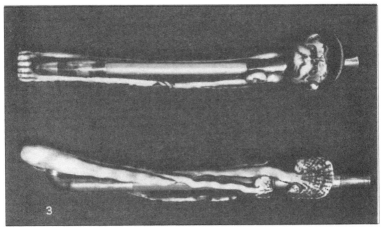

1 and 2. TWO UNUSUAL JAPANESE PIPES
3 and 4. JAPANESE PIPES IN CARVED CASES

PLATE VIII

TWO SIBERIAN PIPES

PLATE X

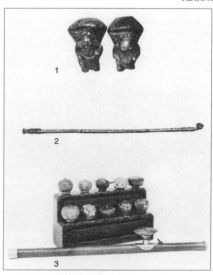

1. TWO KOREAN PIPE BOWLS
2. A WESTERN CHINESE PIPE
3. CHINESE OPIUM PIPE AND BOWLS

life involved incessant movement as the game moved to fresh pastures. These Indians lived in large groups, their hunting life was a dangerous one, and the trespass of one tribe upon the traditional hunting ground of another was an offence that threatened an already precarious livelihood. Hence these were among the most fierce and warlike of the North American Indians, and their organization for peace and war was correspondingly elaborate.

The Omahas were divided into two groups or phratries, the Sky people and the Earth people, representing the Father principle and the Mother principle in life, and this dualism was expressed in many details of their life—*e.g.*, in the arrangement of the camp, in their games, and in their ceremonial. They possessed two sacred council pipes, which were always kept together, and were never separated in any ceremonial use; there were also two war pipes and two peace pipes. The keeper of the sacred pipes and the keeper of the ritual for filling them were both important functionaries who attended the council of chiefs, although without having a voice in its decisions. After the members of the council were in their places, the keeper of the sacred pipes laid these before

the two principal chiefs, who called upon the
keeper of the ritual to prepare them for use. As
he filled them with native tobacco, he intoned in a
low voice the ritual words that belonged to the act.
After the pipes were filled, they were again laid
before the two chiefs, for they were only smoked to
give authority to some decision that had been
arrived at. When the occasion arose, the two

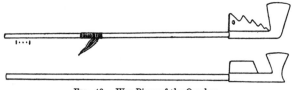

FIG. 48.—War Pipes of the Omahas.

pipes were passed in opposite directions round the
circle, one being handed to the principal chief
sitting towards the north, and the other to the
principal chief sitting towards the south. The
keeper and his assistant took the pipes from
each - smoker to the next, and any mishap was
looked upon as disastrous : it was indeed a sacrilege,
and might cost the careless handler of the pipe his
life. Silence was observed during the smoking.

The war pipes of these people are sketched in
Fig. 48 ; it will be noticed that they are perfectly
plain both as regards bowl and stem. The peace

pipes on the other hand had an elaborately decorated stem, of which that shown in Fig. 49 is a typical example. The character and arrangement of each feather and each tuft of hair was charged with significance, and the peace pipe of any particular tribe was as easily recognizable to other tribes as was the banner or the coat of arms of a feudal lord in olden days in Europe. This

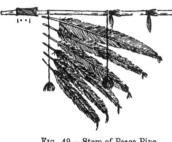

was necessary, for the pipe often served as a pass or safe-conduct for a messenger through hostile country.

FIG. 49.—Stem of Peace Pipe

The ritual meaning of the pipe of peace was soon learned by the early European explorers of America, and they mastered the art of smoking as much from necessity as from inclination. Father Lewis Hennepin, the French friar, who accompanied La Salle, the famous explorer of the Mississippi, into the unknown interior of the Continent, narrates how by this talisman they made their way among the tribes of whose language they knew no word, and speaks of the relief and security they felt when, on one occasion, after a first refusal of the pipe, and after a fierce discussion among some strange Indians, the leading chief at last put it to his lips and their safety was assured. Father Hennepin and La Salle journeyed to the Mississippi by way of the Great Lakes, and were most familiar with the tribes of the Iroquois or Five Nations, whose hunting and fighting grounds formed, as it were, a frontier zone between the early French and early English colonists. The Father's own description of the pipe of peace, written in 1678, is worth quoting at length, for it tallies so exactly with the observations of Catlin made a century and a half later. "We sent three men to buy provisions in the village, with the Calumet or Pipe of Peace which those of the Island [in Lake Huron] had given us. And because the Calumet of Peace is the most sacred thing among the savages, I shall here describe the same. It is a large Tobacco Pipe of a red, black, or white Marble. The head is finely polished. The Quill, which is commonly two foot and a half long, is made of a pretty strong Reed or Cane, adorned with Feathers of all colours, and interlaced with locks of women's hair. Every Nation adorns it as they think fit, and according to the Birds they have in their Country.   Such a Pipe is a safe conduct among all the Allies of the Nation who has given it.   And in all Embassies the Calumet is carried as a symbol of Peace.   The savages being generally persuaded that some great misfortune would befall them if they should violate the public Faith of the Calumet.   They fill this pipe with the best Tobacco they have, and then present it to those with whom they have concluded

FIG. 50.—Pipe Stem of Plains Indian.

any great affair, and then smoke out the same after them."

In the case both of the war and peace pipes the stem itself was a long, slender tube made by removing the pith from an ash stem.   The stems of the pipes used for ordinary pleasurable smoking were often of a much more elaborate character. A typical example is given in Fig. 50.   Here the stem is flat, and the markings upon it form a record of the hunting and fighting exploits of its owner ; similar records were often kept by the Indians on their great buffalo robes, which, like the pipes, were the possession of a lifetime.   The pride taken by the owner in his pipe is witnessed to by the prominent way in which it is usually displayed when an Indian has his portrait taken, as in the famous series of drawings by George Catlin, who visited the Indians of the Missouri Basin early in the nineteenth century, before the tide of white immigration had reached so far west. Catlin, who, as an artist, was a keen observer, thus describes the pipe of Mah-to-toh-pa, one of his sitters: " His pipe was ingeniously carved out of red steatite (or Pipe-stone), the stem of which was 3 feet long and 2 inches wide, made from the stalk of a young ash: about half its length was wound with delicate braids of the porcupine, so ingeniously wrought as to represent figures of men and animals upon it. It was also ornamented with the skins and beaks of woodpeckers' heads, and the hair of the white buffalo's tail. The lower half of the stem was painted red, and on its edges it bore the notches he had recorded for the snows (or years) of his life."

It was Catlin who first described in detail the pipe-stone quarry from which all the Plains Indians got the material for their pipe bowls. Consequently this material, which is a deep, rich red, and takes on a beautiful polish, is usually termed catlinite. Within the quarry and its precincts a "truce of God" was observed: all weapons were laid aside, and the mutually hostile tribes dug out the precious material side by side. The quarry lies in the valley of a head-stream of the Mississippi, some four hundred miles west of the modern city of Minneapolis, and thus at a point very readily accessible from all parts of the plains. The legend concerning it runs somewhat as follows: "The Great Spirit at an ancient period here called the Indian nations together, and standing on the precipice of the red pipe-stone rock broke from its wall a piece and made a huge pipe by turning it in his hands. He smoked it over them, and to the North, the South, the East, and the West. Then he told them that this stone was red; that it was their flesh; that they must use it for their peace pipes; that it belonged to them all; and that the war club and scalping knife must not be raised on its ground. At the last the smoke from his great pipe rolled over them all, and he disappeared in its cloud."

The disturbance of Indian life through the advent of Europeans led to a decay of tradition, and at the time when Catlin visited the pipe quarry, there was a complaint that the truce had been broken, that the Dakotas had seized the

quarry for themselves, and that many tribes could
not obtain the ritual stone. This perhaps explains why the Omahas, when studied by the
Bureau, had peace pipes without any bowls, and
why the medicine man who kept the Mandan
peace pipes, and whose portrait Catlin drew,
carried only the decorated pipe stems. On the
other hand, since it was the stems which bore the
distinctive emblems, while the red bowl was quite
plain, besides being easily detached, broken or
lost, it is easy to understand how the stem might
come quite naturally to symbolize the whole pipe.
However that might be, if a tribe were unable to
visit the quarry themselves, they would be un-
likely to make use of "trade" catlinite for their
ceremonial pipes, for stone thus acquired could
not take on a sacred character. "Trade" tobacco
grown by Europeans is rejected for any formal
smoking by tribes which cling to the old ways,
and among the Tewas, a Pueblo tribe, wild tobacco
is known by the specific name of *Po'ae sa*, which
means "ceremonial tobacco." A Tewa pipe is
called *Sa-ku*, literally "tobacco stone," these being
a people among whom the archaic form of pipe
was the stone tube.

The bowl shown in Fig. 51 is typical of the

peace pipes, as regards its plain shape, simple
ornament, and the projecting "foot," which is a
feature of many long-stemmed pipes that are
smoked with the bowl resting
on the ground. The Dunhill
collection contains numbers of
calumet bowls (not necessarily
peace pipes), some of which
conform to tradition, while

FIG. 51.—Catlinite Bowl of
Peace Pipe.

others present exceptional features. The Indian pipe,
Plate IV. (6), shows a modification identified with
the Chippewa tribe—namely, an ornament behind
the bowl somewhat resembling a balustrade; the
second pipe, with a repetition of the hawk totem, is
also Chippewa. The third bowl in Plate IV. is unusually large, and is cut in hexagonal shape from
green steatite, while it has a base-rest beneath it,
as well as the usual projecting foot. The value
of the first calumet in Plate IV. lies in its
unique polished stem, which is carved with a snake
entwined about it, but the catlinite bowl resembles
the Chippewa type, save that instead of the
"balustrade" ornament, there is a simple flange
pierced at one point, whereby the bowl can be
attached to the stem with a thong or cord. Often
a flange below the stem is developed and pierced

for this purpose. The hard-going involved in a hunter's life must frequently have made a pipe bowl work loose from the stem, which was thrust through the belt. Since the Indian brave invariably carried a tomahawk, it was not unnatural that this weapon

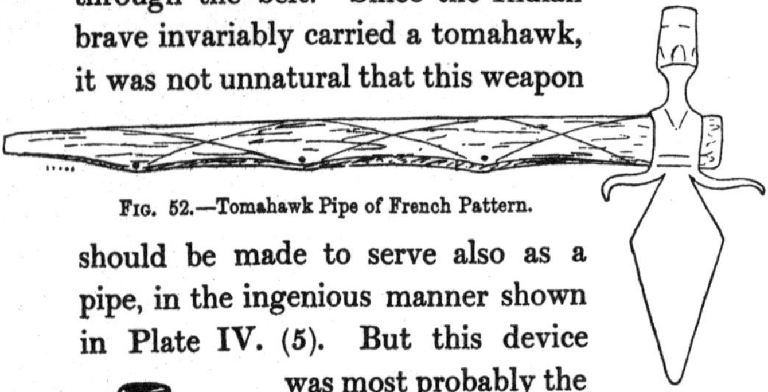

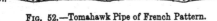

FIG. 52.—Tomahawk Pipe of French Pattern.

should be made to serve also as a pipe, in the ingenious manner shown in Plate IV. (5). But this device was most probably the work, in the first instance, of a European craftsman, for both the English and French supplied the Indians with "trade" tomahawks of steel, since each of these rival nations courted the alliances of the savages. The adaptation of the war-club to serve as a pipe by the Polynesians of the Tonga Islands presents an interesting analogy (Plate IV., 4). Here, of course, smoking is of quite modern intro-duction. French, English, and

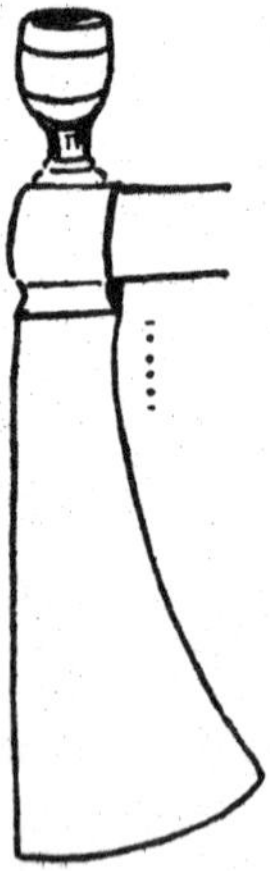

FIG. 53.—Tomahawk Pipe of English Pattern.

Spanish types of tomahawk pipe are shown in Figs. 52, 53, and 54.

A species of Indian pipe magic, by which an erring member of the tribe was doomed, was practised among certain tribes and took place as follows: A tribal pipe was smoked by the leading chief and then passed round the circle. The leading chief then took the cleaning-stick and scraped a little ash on to the ground, saying: "This shall ramble in the calves of his legs" (naming the offender). Again he poured ashes and said: "This shall be for the sinews of his back, and he shall start with pain." Yet a third time he twirled the cleaning-stick, and as the ashes fell to the earth he said: "This for the crown of his head." The belief was that this act finished the man, who must die soon after, just as in mediæval Europe the melting of the waxen image of an enemy upon the fire brought about his untimely death.

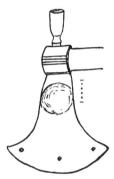

FIG. 54.—Tomahawk Pipe of Spanish Pattern.

A member of John Franklin's Expedition to the Polar Seas (1819-22) gives an interesting account

of the use of the pipe in a ceremony of propitiation
of an idol representing the Deity, which was carried
out by a " brave " who was also a medicine man.
He was a member of the Cree Indian tribe, who
then had hunting grounds in the forests of Sas-
katchewan. The company assembled in a specially
built sweating-house, in the centre of which a
number of red-hot stones were placed and sprinkled
from time to time with water. The resulting
vapour bath would undoubtedly have curative
properties, as the Indians entered the house stark
naked : here again, then, we have the association of
medicine, magic (or religion), and smoking, which
in all probability lies at the root of the custom.
After an invocation to the god, the Indian in
question took up a calumet filled with a mixture
of tobacco and bear-berry leaves, and holding its
stem by the middle, in a horizontal position, over
the hot stones, turned it slowly in a circular manner,
following the course of the sun. Its mouthpiece
being then with much formality held for a few
seconds to the face of the idol, it was next presented
to the earth, having been previously turned a
second time over the hot stones ; and afterwards
with equal ceremony pointed in succession to the
four quarters of the sky ; then, after drawing a few

whiffs from the calumet, the leader handed it to his left-hand neighbour, by whom it was gravely passed round the circle.   When the tobacco was exhausted by passing several times round, the hunter again preferred his urgent requests to the god.   The sweating-house, which was built of branches, was then completely closed with moose-skins, and the worshippers continued their ceremonies within for half an hour, subsequently taking a cold plunge in the river as does the modern bather after a Turkish bath.   The ritual of pointing the pipe to the earth and sky and to the four quarters of the heavens was very commonly observed among the Indians, and suggests a connection with sun-worship, which plays a part in most primitive cults.

A class of Red Indian pipes which are unique in character, differing completely from any met with elsewhere on the Continent, are in use among the fishing tribes of the North-West coast.   Here the environment has special characters of its own : mountains clothed with giant red cedars come down to the very edge of the sea, and the shore is an intricate nexus of quiet fiords, sounds, islands, and islets, much resembling the coast of Norway, although on a far grander scale.   The rivers and fiords teem with salmon, and the sea with halibut, and these Indians get their livelihood from the sea. The forests supply timber for their canoes, and for their well-built dwellings, so that skill in wood-working is part of the normal equipment of every man of the tribe. Wood-carving is an art that is very highly developed, and the favourite subject for the artist is the representation of those members of the animal world which are the totems of his tribe or clan. The great totem poles, set up before the lodges, which serve as family crests or emblems, or as memorials to the past, have often been pictured and described. Besides carving in wood, these Indians work in slate (obtained from Queen Charlotte Island) and in horn, and it is the former that is usually chosen as the material for tobacco pipes. A beautiful specimen from the Dunhill collection shown in Plate V. illustrates the typical features of the peculiar art of the North-West. It will be noticed that the design is one of elaborately interlocked animal and human figures, more regard being paid to the development of a pattern that completely fills the space at the artist's disposal than to any naturalistic representation of the figures depicted. Thus two eyes are inserted in different parts of the carving which are unrelated to any figure, while the wings of the eagle (recognizable by its hooked beak) and the arms of the man in the centre are conventionally disposed.   In this, and in the practice of carving in low relief instead of in the round, the North-Western crafts-man differs entirely from the makers of the earlier mound pipes of the territory to the east of the Rockies.   A very curious feature is the inter-locking of the figures, an animal and a human face often being connected by a protruding tongue.   It is possible that the human faces are those of masked Shamans or priests who in this way hold mystic communication with the animals, which are held to be supernatural beings.   Among the animals, the Sea People, as the Indians call them, naturally form a most important class in the opinion of this sea-fishing race.   Reigning supreme are the killer whales, whose life on the sea-floor is imagined to be the exact counterpart of that of mankind.   The killer whale, or orca, is actually a species of porpoise which competes with the Indians by preying on fish.   Hence it is constantly in their thoughts, and is very frequently depicted on bowls, spoons, etc.

Another pipe shown in Plate V. (Dunhill collection) is a representation of a killer whale carved in the round in wood, and is a very rare and valuable specimen. The exaggerated treatment of the teeth is typical of the native method of emphasizing and conventionalizing some specially important feature of the animal represented. Among other animal totems frequently found on carvings from this locality are the eagle, the raven, the hawk, the beaver, the sea-otter, and the bear. The frog is often used as an ornamental motif. The second slate pipe in Plate V. (Dunhill collection) shows a tiny distorted human mask, with behind it a bird (probably a raven) and two four-footed animal totems. Yet another example in the same plate shows how the artist's skill deserts him when he departs from the traditional subject-matter of his craft, but the representation of the Baptist missionary, side-whiskers, baggy frock-coat, wing-collar, and all, is not without humour.

FIG. 55.—*a*, Eighteenth Century English Clay ; *b*, Indian Pipe based on English Clay.

An exact imitation of the bowl of an eighteenth-century clay pipe in stone, where, however, the " heel " of the clay becomes a pierced flange for securing the bowl to the stem, is a further interesting Dunhill exhibit (Fig. 55), while in the British Museum there is a specimen with a unique stem of grass and carved bowl (Fig. 56).

These North-Western pipes, however, even when carved in purely Indian style, date only from the period of contact with Europeans, for although tobacco was grown, it was not smoked, but chewed, the leaf being pounded first of all with a pestle and mortar, and mixed with lime derived from burnt shells. This method is very reminiscent of the betel-chewing of South-East Asia, as is

FIG. 56.—Indian Pipe with Stem of Grass.

the fact that a kind of poppy was also used as a narcotic. It is possible that Malay or other Asiatic castaways from time to time reached this shore, and introduced their customs, while the lofty ranges of the Rocky Mountains served to isolate the North-West from the rest of America. It is thus highly probable that the first tobacco-pipes which the Indians of this region saw were English or Dutch " clays " traded to them by members of the crews of the *Discovery* and the *Resolution*, the vessels which, under Captain Cook, in 1778, were the first to survey this coast. Since pipe-smoking is here of such recent origin, it naturally plays no part in ceremonial observances : the essential feature of the peace ceremonies of the Tlingits and Haidas, for example, is the scattering of white eagle-down upon the heads of the company, and there is in addition a very elaborate ritual of song and dance.

CHAPTER VI

FAR less is known of the ancient customs and observances of the Indians of South America than of the practices of the races of the Northern Continent. This is largely because the region was left to the Spanish and Portuguese, and did not attract the English, French, and Dutch explorers and pioneers who opened up Canada and the United States. Moreover, the Indians themselves were at a low stage of culture, and when the white men settled along the coast, large numbers were exterminated, or migrated to the interior, while some tribes were converted and Europeanized in the mass by the Jesuit missionaries. The one exceptional race, or rather group of races, inhabiting Peru, and ruled over by the Incas, who were civilized, and practised an advanced agriculture, strangely enough did not use tobacco (except individually in the form of snuff), its place being taken by the leaves of the coca

73

bush (the source of cocaine), which served as a
narcotic and stimulant, and as a preventive of
fatigue. It was characteristic, however, of the
"enlightened despotism" of the Inca, that the
common people, whose lives were regulated down
to the smallest detail, were not allowed the use of
coca. Like the betel leaf in the East, the coca
leaf is mixed with a little lime and chewed, and is
now very generally used in the Andean region. It
is possible that the strain imposed upon the heart
and lungs of dwellers in high mountain regions
prevents them from falling victims to any extent
to the smoking habit. The Tibetans, for example,
although smoking is not unknown to them, prefer
to refresh themselves by drinking tea all day, and
taking snuff; while Mr. Savage Landor considers
that the Abyssinians smoke so little because of
their mountain habitat.

As in Central America, the practices of snuff-
taking and cigar-smoking were found by the
Spaniards among the tribes living on the shores
of the Caribbean Sea, and among those of the
great forests of the Amazon, such methods of
using tobacco being the most suited to the extremely humid climate. It is to this region that
these curious Y-shaped snuff-taking implements

belong, which are made from the slender bones
of birds, capped with hollowed nuts. In some
patterns the two arms are close together and fit
the two nostrils, while in others they are flared
apart to facilitate the important social observance
of mutual snuff-taking. Another Amazonian curiosity is the giant ceremonial cigar, some eighteen
inches long, which is passed from mouth to mouth,
and is so heavy that it must be supported by a
prong during smoking. Peculiar to the North-
West Amazon region is the custom of "tobacco-
licking." When some important matter is to be
engaged upon, for example a war, or a communal
hunting expedition, some tobacco is cooked with
water to a syrup, into which each man dips his
middle finger. The finger is then licked clean,
and all who have thus tasted the tobacco are
bound as by a solemn oath to act together.

To the south of the Selvas or forest area, the
Aruac race is replaced by the Tapuyas, who inhabit
all the rest of Brazil, including the coastal belt,
which was first discovered and settled by the
Portuguese. These people are pipe-smokers, and
the traveller Nieuhoff, who visited Brazil in 1650,
writes of them as follows: "The Brazilians smoke
in pipes made of the shell of a nut, to wit, they

cut a hole in one end of the shell, take out the kernel, and after they have polished them, put a wooden pipe or piece of a reed in the hole. The

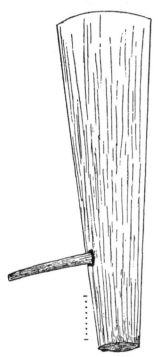

FIG. 57.—Giant Pipe from Upper Amazon Basin.

Tapoyers use very large pipes, made of stone, wood, or clay, the holes of which are so big that they contain a handful of tobacco at a time." The Tupis, a branch of the Tapoyas race, are migratory in their habits, and a Tupi tribe, the Cocamas, is found, far from their original home, in the valleys of the Ucayali and Napo Rivers, which are south-western head-waters of the Amazon system. These people still make and use giant pipes such as Nieuhoff describes, and there are several specimens in the British Museum, of which one is pictured in Fig. 57. They are interesting as showing that the immigrants had adapted the bird-bones, in use locally as snuff-tubes, as the material for their pipe-stems. The bowls are made of hard-wood, abundant, of course, in the forest, and some are slightly ornamented with an incised or stained geometrical pattern. A loosely rolled leaf, and not cut tobacco, is used in this part of the world. Specimens of black pottery bowls in the Museum, such as that in Fig. 58, which come from Para on the Amazon, greatly resemble those of West Africa, a fact which suggests that they were made and used by the Negro slaves and their descendants, who were introduced into the country in large numbers by the Portuguese plantation owners during the late sixteenth and seventeenth centuries.

Fig. 58.—Pottery Bowl from Para.

The Chaco Indians, and those of Paraguay, are great pipe-smokers, but as this region was the scene of the most active labours of the Jesuit missionaries, who gathered the Indians into large villages, and taught them European handicrafts, it is probable that the local pipe-shapes are not indigenous, and possibly the custom itself was of European introduction. Certainly there is no mention of tobacco in the accounts of the earliest exploration of this region. The fact that the word for " pipe " is the same as that for " earth," suggests that the earliest pipes were of pottery, probably with a reed stem. A pipe of crude red pottery, such as

that shown in Fig. 59, is still quite common. The
construction is of the simplest, a slightly tapering
tube of clay being bent up, somewhat after the

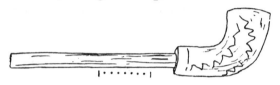

FIG. 59.—Lengua Pottery Pipe.

fashion of the "modified tube" types of the
mound-building Indians. The ornament consists
of a series of incised zigzag lines extremely crude
in character, while the mouthpiece is
of reed. An even more roughly made
specimen, shown in
Fig. 60, is from the
Dunhill collection.

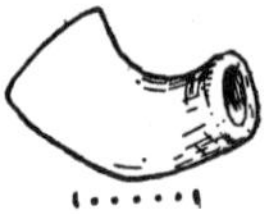

FIG. 60.—Lengua
Pipe Bowl.

From the same tribe, the Lenguas,
who make this pottery pipe, comes
an example of a very curious character carved
out of wood
(Fig. 61): an
upright, flar-

FIG. 61.—Lengua Wooden Pipe.

ing-out bowl rises from the middle of a flat base,
which tapers at either end, the whole being carved
in one piece. Again an inserted reed forms the

mouthpiece. This specimen (British Museum) is marked by the collector as being unusually large but if we turn to a more normal example (Fig. 62) fashioned on similar lines, it seems difficult not to believe that we have here a pipe of which the "normal mound pipe," Fig. 32, is the prototype. In both the bowl rises at right angles from the centre of a symmetrically tapering base or stem,

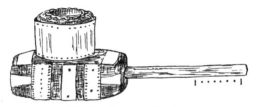

FIG. 62.—Pampas Indian Pipe.

although that carried out in wood has necessarily a thicker base. The simplicity of the South American specimen is obscured by the fact that it is cased and ornamented with brass, while the reed mouthpiece is imitated in brass, and the bowl is lined with metal. It is the work of a Pampas Indian, according to Bragge, from whose collection it is taken, and these Indians are fond of metal ornament, which they use very freely for the trappings of their horses. The Pampas is perhaps a thousand miles from the Chaco region, whence the similar Lengua pipe came, but the intervening country is all open, and is occupied by horse-riding Indians, so that it is probable that the Paraguayan pipe patterns passed southwards.

There is yet a third type of Paraguayan or Chaco pipe that can be related to an archaic North American Indian pattern, although executed in wood, and that is the straight-tube pipe. An example from the Dunhill collection (Fig. 63 *a*) differs only in material from Californian stone

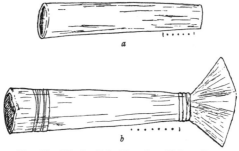

FIG. 63.—Wooden Tube Pipes from El Gran Chaco.

specimens. The second example (Fig. 63 *b*) is about four inches long, but the size may vary from three to six inches, the distinguishing feature here being the flat "fishtail" mouthpiece, which was found in the slate mound pipe of Fig. 33. A curious modification, looking more like a whistle than a pipe, is shown in Fig. 64, where one end of the tube is bowl-shaped.

It is always difficult to draw a hard-and-fast line between a straight pipe and a cigar-holder, but

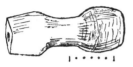

FIG. 64.—Wooden Tube Pipe of Curious Design.

perhaps the latter name should be given to the large wooden tube, with flattened mouthpiece, shown in Fig. 65, for it is used in Paraguay for smoking a decidedly cigar-like roll of tobacco. This, too, might well be an ancient Mexican pipe form, introduced by the Spaniards. Chiefs' pipes are also of the straight variety, although much larger than the common

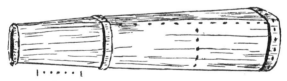

FIG. 65.—Great Wooden Pipe or Cigar Holder.

pipes. They are elaborately decorated, usually with animal figures—*e.g.*, the serpent in the sketch (Fig. 66)—and are used for smoking a loose roll of tobacco leaves.

The series of different types from this prolific region is not yet exhausted, for the pipe in Fig. 67 *a* differs from any yet described. It may perhaps be looked upon as indigenous, or rather as derived

FIG. 66.—Paraguay Chief's Pipe.

from the indigenous Brazilian type, where the mouthpiece is thrust straight into an upright hollow bowl as described by Nieuhoff. This particular specimen is crudely carved in human form, but animal figures are also common. With it may be classed the curiously carved pipe from Matto Grosso, a region lying much further north, near the Selvas, also shown in Fig. 67 b, which is of the same type as the simpler

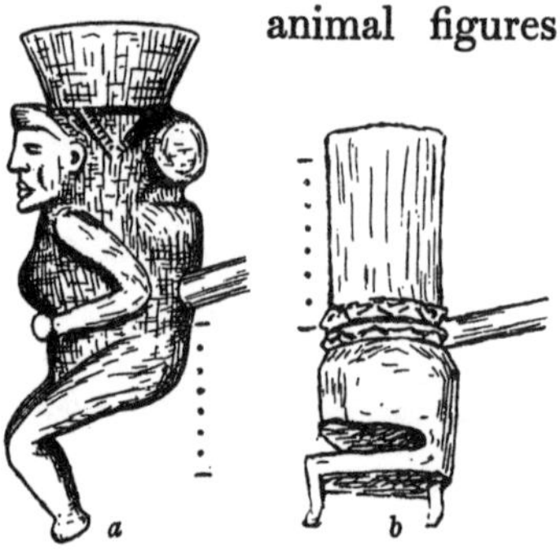

FIG. 67.—Indigenous South American Pipes.

Dunhill specimen in Fig. 68.

The last Paraguay specimen (Fig. 69) is of buff-coloured pottery, in form and size, although not in the detail of the ornament, resembling the Amazon bowls already ascribed to Negro influence. Thus, no one of the pipes of this part of South America is unique in style, so that the suggestion that here the use of tobacco is subsequent to the *Discovery* appears to be well-founded. The Dunhill collection includes a small

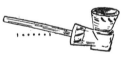

black pottery pipe with a short

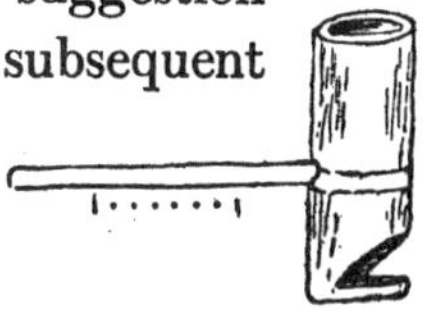

FIG. 68.—Matto Grosso Pipe.

inserted reed stem (Fig. 70), which differs decidedly from the Amazonian and Chaco pottery pipes, being

FIG. 69.—Buff Pottery Pipe, Paraguay.

of the type classed by McGuire (the American authority) as biconical—*i.e.*, a pattern based on two cones set apex to apex at right angles, one forming the bowl, the other receiving the stem. In this case a block-like "heel" masks the joining of the cone. There is some crude attempt at raised ornament. The pipe was the property of an old

FIG. 70.—Slave Woman's Pipe, Peru.

woman who had been a slave in Peru, and was emancipated in 1889.

CHAPTER VII

THE Red Indians of North America did not occupy the country that lay beyond the limits of tree-growth to the north, for the bark of the birch tree, from which they made not only their canoes, but their tepees, their household utensils, and the frames of their snow-shoes, was essential to their mode of life. Thus the barren lands and tundras of the Arctic margins, and the ice-deserts of the islands still further north, were left to the Eskimo, and between the two races there was a feeling of deep distrust and hostility, so that the customs of the one remained quite distinct from those of the other. Hence the Eskimo did not learn pipe-smoking from the Indians, and in the case of the Eastern Eskimo, smoking was unknown until introduced by whale-fishers and other European visitors to the Far North. The Western Eskimo, however, have long been in contact with the peoples of Asia, for the narrow Behring Strait is frozen over during

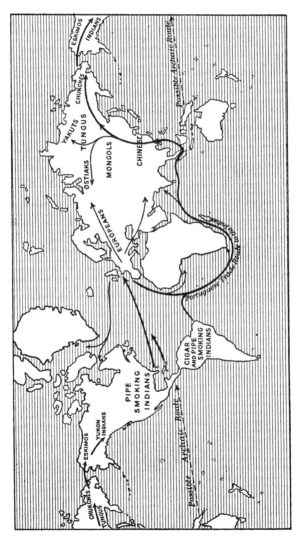

Fig. 71.—How the Pipe went round the World.

the winter months, nor does it even in summer
present an impassable barrier to these intrepid
fishermen in their skin canoes. A comparison of
pipe shapes suggests that the Eskimo learnt
smoking from the Chukches, the aborigines of
the north-eastern Arctic margin of Asia; these
Chukches in their turn had learned the practice
from the Tungus, a race of hunters inhabiting the
forests of the Amur Basin lying to the south, while
the Tungus had learned it from their own southern
neighbours the Mongols and Chinese, to whom they
are racially akin, and whose merchants from very
early times had visited their territory to purchase
furs. As the practice reached the Chinese during
the sixteenth century through the intermediary of
Europeans, who themselves had acquired it earlier
in that century from the Red Indians, the pipe had
made the complete circuit of the world before it
became known to the Eskimo, although their home
lay in the continent that had given both pipes and
tobacco to the world. Nor is the story quite complete, for, curiously enough, since European penetration has brought peace between the native races
of America, the Eskimo have passed the custom
on to a hitherto non-smoking Indian tribe in the
Yukon district. Thus the full circle, from Indian

round to Indian again, has been accomplished.   A
graphic version of the story is given by the map
(Fig. 71) facing page 84.

The distinguishing characters of Eastern Asiatic,
and consequently also of Western Eskimo pipe-
smoking, are the
use of a very small
bowl, which is
smoked out in a
few whiffs, and

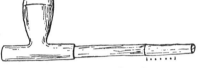

FIG. 72.—Eastern Eskimo Pipe.

the practice of very deep inhalation of the smoke,
so that these few whiffs produce a condition of
well-nigh intoxication.   The Eastern Eskimo and
Greenland Eskimo, on the other hand, use large-
bowled pipes, which are smoked in the ordinary
way.   Fig. 72 shows a Hudson Bay (Eastern)

Eskimo pipe, the
bowl carved from
green   mottled
stone, with a stem
of   wood   and   a

FIG. 73.—Greenland Eskimo Pipe.

mouthpiece of brass.   The projecting "foot" in
front of the bowl shows Red Indian influence, for
the pipe is modern, and the races are now in contact, but the Greenland pipe in Fig. 73 is a purely
European type, although executed in stone.

A characteristic Western Eskimo pipe is shown
in Fig. 74. The bowl is carved from stone, and
has a wide rim round the tiny orifice: two flanges

FIG. 74.—Western Eskimo Pipe: Stone Bowl.

at the base of the bowl allow it to be lashed with
raw-hide to the stem, which is made from a naturally curved and tapering piece of wood. The wood
has been split for the purpose of making the bore,
and has then been lashed together again with the
thong of seal-skin or walrus-hide that takes the

FIG. 75.—Western Eskimo Pipe: Metal Bowl.

place of string or wire among these people. This
standard pattern is seen in the pipe in Fig. 75, but
in this case the curvature of the stem is more

marked, and the bowl is of white metal, with a
large flat disc serving as rim: it is lashed to the
stem in exactly the same manner as the stone bowl.
Pipes in the Dunhill collection showing similar
features are shown in Plate VI.   One of the
specimens has a greenstone bowl of unusual
pattern, lacking the wide rim, although it has both
the tiny interior dimensions, and the flanges for
lashing it to the stem, that are characteristic of the
area.   A typical Chukche pipe, an example col-

FIG. 76.—Chukche Pipe (after Nordenskiold).

lected by Nordenskiold during the voyage of the
Vega, is shown in Fig. 76 ; it is only necessary to
glance at it to accept the Asiatic origin of these
Eskimo pipes.   The Eskimo, however, is not seen
at his best as a worker in wood or metal, for such
materials are scarce and poor in his environment ;
all his more precious possessions and *objets d'art*
are fashioned from the finest material he has at his
command, which is walrus ivory.   Three ivory pipes
(Plates VI. and VII.) are among the gems of the
Dunhill collection, being far more beautifully

executed even than those to be seen in the British Museum. On one side of the first (Plate VI., 3) the artist has depicted the return of a sledging party, who have had a "good hunting," to judge by the way in which a man is pushing behind each sledge to help the dog teams. The women and children have rushed shouting from the igloo, or ice-hut, and greetings are being exchanged. To the right, beneath the pipe-bowl, are shown a number of seals, one of which has been caught by a hunter, who is dragging it along on its back. Just below this picture three men have left their sledge to chase a dog which has made off with their catch, and one of them is in the act of delivering a mighty kick to the culprit. On the reverse side of the pipe are summer hunting scenes, which take place further inland on the margin of the tundra, as indicated by the few dwarfed trees. One of the Eskimo is seen stalking a caribou (the American reindeer) with his bow and arrow, while others are hunting foxes (to be distinguished from the dogs by their bushy tails, which are held out straight, instead of being curled over the back). The little thumbnail sketches of men and moons date the various incidents which the pipe-maker wishes to record. This pipe is from Behring Straits. The second

pipe, from Norton Sound, shows some fine carving
in the round.   A human figure is seen struggling
with a walrus, which is held firmly by the tusks,
while behind are two living seals, and one dead
(turned on its back).   The sides of the pipe are
delicately engraved with wonderfully realistic representations of the characteristic Arctic animals,
including seals, walrus, the sea-otter, and a number
of salmon.   The bowl is of peculiar interest, representing as it does a two-headed bear lying on its
back : the bear is one of the chief totem animals of
the Eskimo (their system strongly resembling that
of the North-Western Indian tribes), and it was
probably the family emblem of the owner or maker
of the pipe.   The third pipe (Plate VII.) shows
European contact : a house with chimneys, a flag-
staff, a herd of tame reindeer, and a large fishing
net in use behind the igloo.   The boring of the
ivory stem has been effected by cutting out from
beneath the stem a series of oblong panels, which
are subsequently fitted back into place : this
method, as will be presently shown, is of Siberian
origin.   It allows the pipe to be cleaned by the
removal of a panel, just as the wooden-stemmed
pipe can be cleaned by unlashing the two segments.
The foul, oily refuse taken from the pipe-stem is

actually eaten by the Eskimo, and the strength of
his stomach is shown also by the fact that when
chewing tobacco he swallows the saliva instead of
expectorating. The practice of putting a tiny
tuft of dog's hair at the bottom of the pipe-bowl
is said to make the tobacco more pungent, and
many smokers consequently attach a piece of dog-
skin to the pipe-stem (see the Dunhill pipe in
Plate VI.), and this, too has been learned from

FIG. 77.—Eskimo Drawing of Pipe Smokers.

Siberia, where, however, the hair of the reindeer is
substituted, that being the animal with which the
Northern Asiatics are daily in contact.

Since the Eskimo are such inveterate smokers,
as Captain Cook was not slow to observe when he
visited the Aleutian Islands, the clever drawings
which these people scratch on ivory or bone often
depict them thus employed. The facsimile in
Fig. 77 shows a village scene, with four smokers
seated upon the ground in various comfortable
attitudes between two igloos, or winter huts. The
smoker on the right is being handed his skin
tobacco bag by his wife, while his little child is

begging for a whiff. The mode of entering the
low door of the igloo on all fours is amusingly
shown in this drawing. The next picture (Fig. 78)
shows a man resting on the edge of his sledge

while enjoying a pipe, and
the third (Fig. 79) shows a
smoker taking his ease on
a sloping bank as he criti-
cally watches two friends

FIG. 78.—Eskimo Drawing of
Pipe Smoker.

creep warily towards a wounded reindeer, which
seems likely to turn at bay. This Eskimo is
smoking a pipe of a pattern that has not so far been
described, the stem being curved out into the shape
of a duck's breast beneath the bowl. This is yet
another easily recognized Siberian pattern, a simple

FIG. 79.—Eskimo Drawing of Smoker with " Duck's Breast " Pipe.

example being shown in Fig. 80 a, which is taken
from Tiedemann's " Geschichte des Tabaks," where
the pipe is described on the authority of Lutke as
being made of clay and used by the Chukches.

A more elaborate specimen, made of wood inlaid
with white metal, and having a metal bowl, is also
shown in Fig. 80 b. This is an Ostiak pipe, the

Ostiaks being a heathen tribe inhabiting the
Siberian forests rather to the west of the home of
the Tungus, with whom, however, as well as with
the Chukches, they are in contact.   The stem, as
the drawing shows, has an oblong panel cut out
and replaced after the manner of the walrus ivory
pipes, and in the big hollow beneath the bowl fine

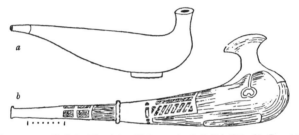

FIG. 80.—*a*, Chukche Pipe (after Tiedemann) ; *b*, Ostiak " Duck's Breast "
Pipe of Wood and Metal.

shavings are packed which absorb the oils and
juices from the tobacco and can be removed for
chewing.   It is probably a pipe of this " duck's
breast" pattern that is described as being in use
among the Ostiaks by the Russian envoy, Ysbrants
Ides.   Ides was sent by Peter the Great across
Siberia on an embassy to the Emperor of China,
and we owe to him much curious and interesting
information about the native races of Siberia at the
close of the seventeenth century.   The passage

about the Ostiak smokers is as follows : " To smoke tobacco, to which all, both men and women, are very much addicted, instead of pipes they use a stone kettle, in which they stick a pipe made for that purpose, and at two or three drawings, after they have taken some water in their mouths, can suck out the whole pipe ; and they swallow the smoak, after which they fall down and lie insensible like dead men, with distorted eyes, both hands and feet trembling for about half an hour. They foam at the mouth, so that they fall into a sort of epilepsy, and we could not observe where the smoak vented itself, and in this manner several of them are lost. For as they are on the water travelling, or sitting by the fire, some of these violent smoakers fall into the water and are drowned, or into the fire and are burned, but some after they have sucked the smoak, let it out at their throats again, and these are in better condition than the others." The reference here to the deep inhalation, already mentioned as characteristic of Asiatic smoking as learned from the Chinese, is especially interesting.

Just as walrus ivory is the favourite medium for artistic expression among the Eskimo, so is fossil mammoth ivory among the tribes of Northern

Siberia, and the British Museum has several examples of pipes made from this material, of which one is shown in Fig. 81, while two very fine ones, one mounted in metal, are included in the

FIG. 81.—Mammoth Ivory Pipe: Native Pattern.

Dunhill collection (Plates VI. and VII.). The bowl and stem are all in one, but the mouthpiece is detachable: the hollow of the bowl is lined with metal, and is of the usual very small size, with a wide rim or flange of ivory around it. The stem is bored straight through from end to end, and the front

FIG. 82.—Copy of Mammoth Ivory Pipe in Metal and Wood.

opening is subsequently plugged up as the sectional diagram shows. Fig. 82 shows a pipe which is an exact copy of the mammoth ivory pipe, but which is made entirely of white metal, save that the mouthpiece is of wood inlaid with white metal after the Russian style. The reproduction of a shape which has been determined by the original material used, in a material which would really lend itself to a more useful pattern, is a commonplace of primitive craftsmanship. In this case a natural shoot of soft wood possibly determined the original pattern, which was imitated in mammoth ivory, and so became the stereotyped pipe-pattern for the region. Hence, when the metal-worker set out to make a pipe, he used metal to make an ivory pipe in facsimile. The resemblance in size and shape between these pipes and the wooden ones made from a natural twig by the Ainus (see Plate XI.) is certainly remarkable, although it may be merely a coincidence.

Russian influence has naturally made itself felt throughout Siberia, for the

Fɪɢ. 83.—Mammoth Ivory Pipe : Russian Pattern.

Russians had crossed right to the Pacific by the middle of the seventeenth century, and this finds expression in the pipe shapes. Thus Fig. 83 shows

a pipe in the Russian style carved from mammoth
ivory, which was bought from the mouth of a
Yakut woman in the Lena valley, just south of
the Arctic circle, by Mr. Bassett Digby. The
pipes in Fig. 84 are also from Mr. Digby's collection. One is of mammoth ivory carved to
imitate a cask; the other, crudely hacked from
wood, is a rough imitation of a Western European
briar. The latter, according to Mr. Digby, is

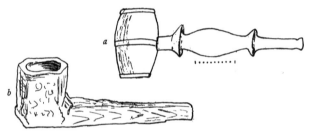

FIG. 84.—a, Mammoth Ivory Pipe : Russian Influence ; b, Siberian
Pipe of roughly-carved Wood.

smoked by Russians and white Siberians, if a
pipe is used at all, but the cigarette is practically
universal.

Fig. 85 shows a Tungus pipe of wood and white
metal, with a large bowl of purely Russian pattern,
while Fig. 86 shows a simpler wooden pipe of a
similar character, the bowl crudely lined with tin.
Fig. 87 shows another Tungus pipe, the bowl of

which is an exact copy of the tiny Chinese pattern, executed in bone, however, instead of in metal as the Chinese make it; it is lashed to the split stem with a hide thong, after the manner of the Chukche or Eskimo pipe. Beneath it is a crude copy of a Chinese

FIG. 85.—Tungus Pipe of Wood and Metal: Russian Bowl.

pipe carried out entirely in metal, a type which is often used by the Tungus.

Two Siberian pipes in the Russian style (Dunhill collection) are shown in Plate VIII. The metal work, and the well-made wooden stems, are characteristic of this area.

FIG. 86.—Tungus Pipe: Russian Style.

The passionate fondness which these northern peoples display for tobacco is probably a result of the extreme hardship of their lives in such a severe climate. Nordenskiold even describes an unweaned Chukche child (who was, however, of an age to walk) as both smoking and chewing tobacco. Since in these remote parts of Asia tobacco is only procured by barter from the Russians or from the Chinese, it is commonly adulterated with slivers of wood, and the fact that

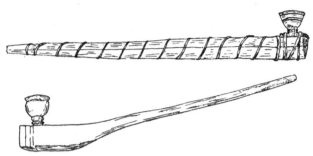

FIG. 87.—Tungus Pipes: Chinese Style.

the same method and exact proportion of adulteration is practised by the Eskimo as by the Siberians is further evidence that the smoking customs of the former come from the neighbouring continent. Nowadays, of course, since the penetration of Alaska the Western Eskimo have come into possession of European pipes, and copy their patterns.

FIG. 88.—Walrus Ivory Pipe: European Style.

An example executed in ivory with a wooden mouthpiece is shown in Fig. 88; it came from Behring Strait. Similarly, the modern Ainus and the Gilyaks make crude wooden pipes (Fig. 89) resembling the cheap French cherry-wood type. The Gilyaks are a fishing people who are neighbours of the Ainu in Saghalien, and are found also

FIG. 89.—Ainu and Gilyak Pipes: European Style.

in the Amur River; the second pipe sketched in Fig. 89 is curious in that the angle between the bowl and stem is greater than a right angle, a very unusual occurrence, since it brings the bowl into an awkward position.

CHAPTER VIII

IT is difficult to believe that the Europeans, when they reached the Far East in the sixteenth century, had anything new to teach the age-long cultured races of China and Japan, of whose wealth and wisdom glowing accounts had been current in the Western World since the return of Messer Marco Polo from the court of the Grand Khan nearly three hundred years earlier. Yet native historians are unanimous in declaring that tobacco and tobacco-smoking was a new thing appearing practically simultaneously in China, Japan, Persia, and India towards the close of the century that saw the Portuguese in power in the Indian Seas. The Portuguese and Spanish sailors and adventurers, familiar with the West Indies, probably smoked cigars as a rule, and this form of smoking is now almost exclusively followed in some parts of tropical Asia, as, for example, Java and Burma, for it is suitable to the hot, moist climate, but the

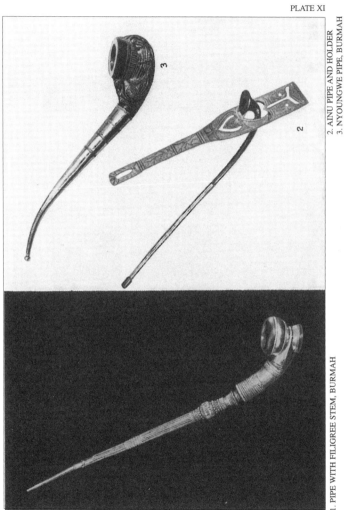

PLATE XI

1. PIPE WITH FILIGREE STEM, BURMAH

2. AINU PIPE AND HOLDER
3. NYOUNGWE PIPE, BURMAH

PLATE XII

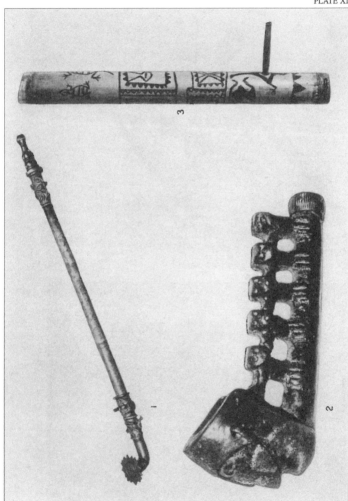

1. PIPE FROM BRUNEI
2. BOWL OF ANGAMI NAGA PIPE
3. PAPUAN PIPE

PLATE XIII

1. NARGILEH   2. MOUNTED NARGILEH

PLATE XIV

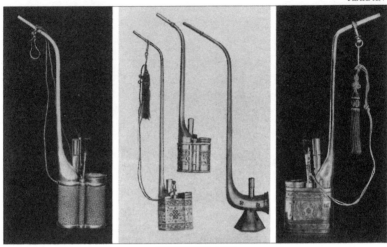

CHINESE WATER-PIPES

PLATE XV

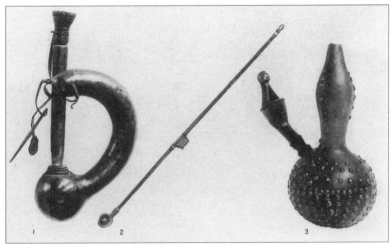

1. BANZA WATER-PIPE
2. TURKISH CHIBOUVE
3. GOURD PIPE WITH WIND SHIELD, CONGO

PLATE XVI

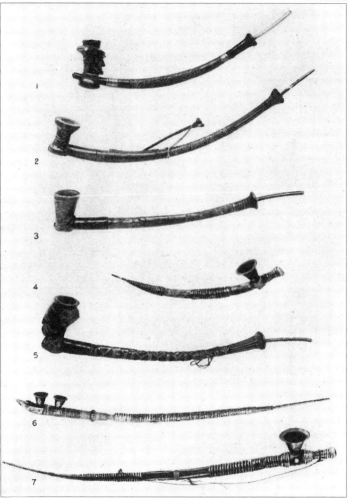

1, 2, 3 AND 5. PIPES OF BUSHONGO AND NEIGHBOURING TRIBES
4, 6 and 7. MONBUTTU PIPES, BOUND WITH COPPER

PLATE XVII

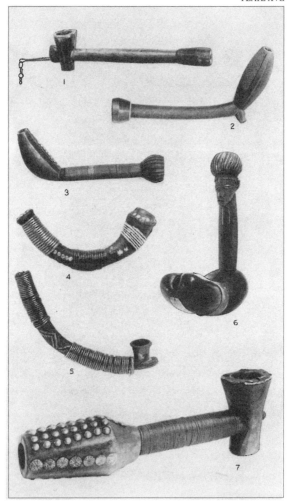

1. PIPE FROM KASAI RIVER
2, 3 and 6. PIPES FROM UPPER
   UBANGHI AND WELLE RIVERS
4 and 5. PIPES FROM UBANGHI
   RIVER DISTRICT
7. PIPE FROM BASOKO

PLATE XVIII

1. CHIEF'S PIPE, DAHOMEY
2. METAL PIPE BOWL, ASHANTI
3 and 4. BALI FETISH PIPES

PLATE XIX

1. BUAKA PIPE   2. BALUBA PIPE   3. LOANGO PIPE

All with female figures

Portuguese were familiar with the pipe in Brazil, and it may be that a simple Brazilian shape—as for example the hollow nut, with a straight reed or cane stem—was the prototype of all Far Eastern pipes.

One of the first steps taken by the Portuguese after Vasco da Gama's historic voyage was to possess themselves of all the Arab trading stations round the Arabian Sea, including Sofala, Mombasa, and Ormuz. The Arabs of these towns and their negro associates thus soon learned the use of tobacco, which was especially welcome to Moham-medans who were forbidden wine, and the Arab sailors must have been active in spreading the custom in all the ports which they frequented. Tobacco was soon found to be an acceptable and easily handled article of trade, and the Portuguese brought it from their Brazilian plantations and planted it also at their refreshing stations on the sea-route to the East. It was not to their interest, however, that planting should spread to Asia, and for some time smoking must have been confined to the well-to-do of the more or less cosmopolitan seaports.

English sailors became smokers in the last quarter of the sixteenth century, and as at about this time trade relations were opened up with Russia, the Levant, and Persia, it is reasonable to suppose that the English brought the pipe into the Near East while the Portuguese still maintained their policy of exclusion in India. Dutch seamen were deeply occupied in home and in Arctic waters at this critical period, and a Delft physician, writing to Neander (the author of " Tobacologia "), observes that he first saw cigar and pipe-smoking at the University of Leyden in 1590, where the fashion was introduced by French and English students. Within a dozen years the English and Dutch had successfully challenged the Portuguese monopoly in the East, and had founded their East India Companies, and whether they introduced the seeds or not, it is significant that the cultivation of tobacco in India, China, and Japan was begun just about this time. Certainly neither nation was interested in preventing such development, for as yet neither had plantations of their own.

Historians give 1605 as the first year in which tobacco-growing is actually mentioned as going on in India, and the same date is given for Japan. In 1607 a Nagasaki doctor named Saka writes as follows : " Of late a new thing is come into fashion called tobacco (the Japanese use the same word

' tobako '), it consists of large leaves which are cut up and of which one drinks the smoke." In 1612 the smoking and planting of tobacco was sufficiently important in China (where Amoy was the centre of dispersal) to call forth an Imperial Edict forbidding it, just as the Emperor Jehangir, with equal lack of success, forbade it in India in 1617. Two years previously, Sir Thomas Roe, the English Ambassador to the Mogul's Court, had remarked of the Indians: " They sow tobacco in vast plenty, and smoak it as much."

The Japanese were responsible for the almost immediate introduction of tobacco into Korea, and as they described it as a plant brought to them by the " Namban," that is to say the Southern Barbarians, for so they termed the Europeans, the Koreans called it "nambanpoy." About fifty years later, the French traveller, Henri Hemel, who spent some time in Korea, remarked on the popularity of tobacco: " They take so much at present that there are very few of either sex but what smoke, and the very children practise it at four or five years of age." Such a statement may be natural exaggeration, but it shows that here as well as elsewhere smoking supplied an almost universal human need for a mild narcotic. Eastern people were, of course, already familiar with such opiates as opium, bang, and hashish, which were taken through the mouth, but their harmful properties were recognized, and their use was confined to a very small proportion of the population. Opium smoking, as a definite habit, did not become widespread until the early eighteenth century.

Since the Chinese policy of exclusiveness kept actual intercourse with Europeans within very narrow limits, and the success of the Jesuit Missions led alarmed Japan to close her country absolutely against the " Southern Barbarians " in the middle of the seventeenth century, it is natural that the pattern of pipe evolved in these countries should have some unique characteristics. The practice that soon arose of mixing a little opium with the tobacco determined that the size of the

bowl should be very small, and in shape and size it resembles an acorn cup ; the

FIG. 90.—Typical Japanese Pipe.

stem is of cane, and is therefore quite straight, and is set in at right angles to the bowl, which is usually of metal. The Japanese pipes (Fig. 90) are decidedly smaller and daintier than the Chinese, and the tiny ball of fine-cut tobacco which the bowl holds is exhausted in a few whiffs. The pipes of both nations are often beautifully chased and ornamented, various metals and such materials as ivory, jade, and lacquer being introduced into the workmanship. The pipe is kept in an elaborate case, embroidered, carved or lacquered, which is hung from the girdle to which it is fastened in Japan by a *netzuke*, or elaborately carved ivory toggle (Plate IX.). It is said that the earliest Japanese pipes were of great size, and were stuck in the belt like a sword; if this was so it lends point to the foremost of the " Disadvantages of Smoking" alleged by an old Japanese author, to wit: " There is a natural tendency to hit people over the head with one's pipe in a fit of anger," but on the contrary side he sets down among the " Advantages": " It is a companion in solitude; it is a store-house for reflection, and gives time for the fumes of wrath to disperse." An unusually large and heavy Japanese pipe, the elaborately chased and ornamented stem of which is made of iron, is to be seen in the Dunhill collection (Plate IX., 1) and is described as being the type favoured by wrestlers and other persons of a Bohemian way of life.

The Chinese and Korean pipes are to be distinguished from the Japanese as well by the detail of their workmanship and ornament as by their greater size, as may be seen in the example from the Dunhill collection shown in Plate X. Mr. Lowell, an American who visited Korea in the eighties, says: " We leaned back in our chairs and the attendants lit for us our pipes. This service was hardly so gratuitous a luxury as it sounds. The pipes were a yard long, and it was only just within bounds of possibility to light them one's self. . . . The pipes were made of slender bamboo fitted with brass bowls and mouth-pieces, finished to resemble silver. Though of the same form, it is much more nearly a full blown specimen of the pipe than the Japanese is ; and what is especially pleasing, the bowls are much larger, so that one has not to be knocking out the ashes and refilling them." In the illustrations to Hamel's travels, already referred to, the Koreans are represented with very long-stemmed pipes, which confirms the suggestion that such was the original Japanese pipe.

Two carved wooden pipe-bowls from Korea (Plate X.), representing the figures of priests, show a complete departure from the type-form of the area, since their general contour and proportions are based on those of the opium bowl (Plate X.), although instead of the pinhole on which the tiny ball of opium is placed, there is a hollow sufficiently large to take the customary "fill" of tobacco. Besides the Chinese pipe with the little cup-shaped bowl, one with a cone-shaped bowl is also in common use, frequently with an all-metal stem.

It has already been noted that the Sino-Japanese or miniature type of bowl has passed into the interior of Asia and Siberia, and it is interesting to find that in regions where, owing to the climate, bamboo is no

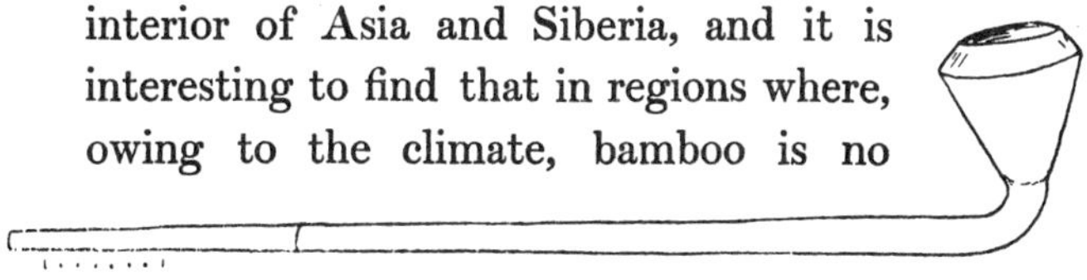

FIG. 91.—Metal Pipe from Bhutan.

longer available, the stem is often made entirely of metal. Such metal pipes are smoked by the Tungus, by the Buryats of Mongolia, by the people of Bhutan (see Fig. 91), where, however, local circumstances dictate a larger bowl, and by the Tibetans. They have the special advantage of "lasting a lifetime," and so are suitable for people who are snow-bound in winter, or who may be nomads wandering through a desolate country far

from any market or bazaar. The ritual act of
hospitality in Tibet is the offer of tea, everyone
carrying his own wooden cup at his belt, but,
in addition, the exchange of snuff-boxes or of
tobacco pouches is an essential part of the welcome of a stranger to the nomad's tent, and it
is accompanied by the exchange of stereotyped
phrases of courtesy, with reference to the pastures
and the cattle with which all pastoral people are
naturally preoccupied. The Ainu, who must have
learned smoking from the Japanese, make the
"natural" wooden pipe already described in
Chapter II., the resemblance to Japanese pipes
being merely in the tiny size of the hole cut for
the tobacco. These people are neither potters nor
metal-workers, wood and bark being their commonest working materials. They have a unique
custom of making a wooden frame to support the
pipe during smoking, as shown in the illustration
(Plate XI.), the purpose being possibly to pro-
tect their long curly beards which distinguish them
so remarkably from the smooth-faced Mongols.
They are very proud of these beards, and make use
of an implement like a carved wooden paper-knife
to lift their moustaches when drinking.

The different Chinese types of pipe-bowls are

used also in French Indo-China and Siam, but here, as in Burmah, Ceylon, and a great part of Malaysia, betel - chewing, varied by cigar and cigarette smoking, holds the first place. Pipe-smoking is, however, common among the less cultured peoples who occupy the rougher country, as for example the Moi of the interior of South Annam, who make either metal pipes on

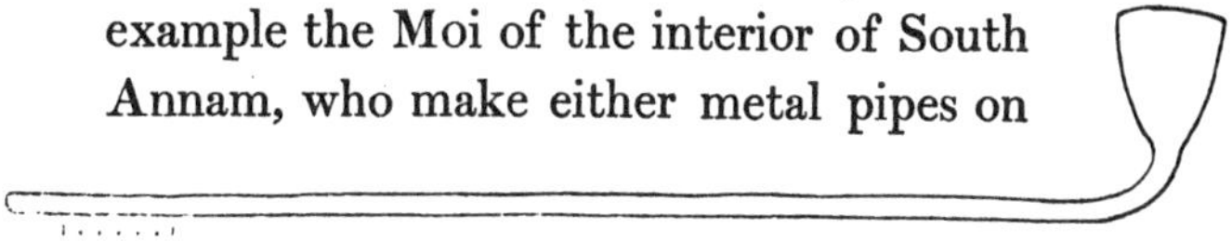

FIG. 92.—Moi Metal Pipe : Annam.

the Chinese conical bowl pattern (Fig. 92), or a cane and bamboo pipe of which the Chinese is again the prototype (see Fig. 93). The Karens of Lower Burmah also make a very simple pipe from a naturally or artificially curved

FIG. 93.—Moi Pipes of Wood and Cane.

cane into which a more slender cane is inserted as mouthpiece, as shown in Fig. 94 : a variant with a more developed bowl is shown beside it, while

Fig. 95 shows a pipe of the same shape and proportions as the common model, but very much smaller, and elaborately decorated with brass wire, brass rings, and tiny inlaid dots of metal. A tiny cone of metal (shown

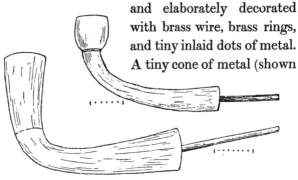

FIG. 94.—Karens Pipes.

separately) protects the inside of the bowl, and in this case the pipe itself is of some dark hardwood.

From the Shan States in Eastern Burmah come the mysterious Nyoungwe pipes, so called because their pottery bowls are dug up near the town of that name, and are not fashioned by the people who

FIG. 95.—Karens Pipe, ornamented with Brass.

smoke them. The records of Nyoungwe go back to the fifteenth century, but who were the people who actually made these bowls in the past is not known. They are greatly prized, being used as touchstones for testing gold, and they are often remounted very elaborately by their finders. Their characteristic shape, and their conventional pinnate ornament, with three or more lobes embracing

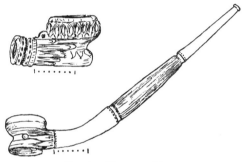

FIG. 96.—Nyoungwe Pipes.

the bowl, are shown in the examples in Fig. 96. This ornament is considered to be the conventionalized representation of the wings of a bird, and this adds great interest to the specimen in the Dunhill collection (Plate XI., 3), where the complete form of a bird (probably a peacock) is shown, the pin-feathers of the wing pointing towards the bowl, and the long tail completely embracing it, while the head faces the smoker. The specimen in Fig. 97, which came from the

Khyens of Western Burmah, shows very clearly
the conventionalizing of a "wing" pattern. In this
particular case the pottery bowl is rather crudely
affixed with a lump of wax to the bamboo stem,
which is fitted with a plain metal mouthpiece. The
people of the Shan States still make pottery bowls

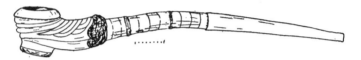

FIG. 97.—Khyens Pipe: Nyoungwe Pattern.

of the same general shape and character as the
Nyoungwe pipes, with elaborate representations
(often grotesque) of animal and human figures
designed so as to embrace the cup-shaped bowl.
The stem is usually curved in, so as to lie at an
acute angle to the bowl, and this is characteristic

also of the metal pipes of the
region of which Fig. 98 shows
the base-type. Here the bowl is
thimble-shaped, and not cup-
shaped, and has a distinct base
or foot, while the ornament is
of fine wire. Elaborate examples decorated with
filigree work are made, of which that in Plate XI.
(Dunhill collection) is a good specimen, although

FIG. 98.—Metal Pipe:
Shan States.

here the bowl is lined with black pottery. Also
from the Dunhill collection is a unique Angami
Naga pipe (Plate XII.), in which the cone-shaped
bowl (with the rim, as usual in this region, slightly
higher in front) is carved into a human head, and
behind it are seated in a linked row five grotesque
figures which have some mystic significance. It may be compared with the
British Museum specimen in Fig. 99
belonging to a chief of a Naga tribe of

FIG. 99.—Naga Chief's Pipe.

the Patkoi Mountains. Here the resemblance to
a human head is very rude, but the face is covered
with dots, the "ako" of the owner, showing his
success as a hunter or warrior. This pipe is unusually large (about 15 inches long), and the cane
mouthpiece is attached by bands of plaited split
rattan, coloured red. The bowl, which preserves
the typical outline (apart from the carving)
associated with this region, is further ornamented
with strings of tiny beads and tassels. A wooden
bowl with an upward slanting rim is used by the
Abors, a tribe of the Himalaya slopes of Assam,

but in the specimen shown (Fig. 100) the stem is
directly inserted in the bowl.   This stem is of cane,
silver-mounted, with a " twin-bulb " ornament on
the silver mouthpiece.   A similar mouthpiece
is seen in the
Assam pipe,
Fig. 101, but
here the bowl
is Chinese.

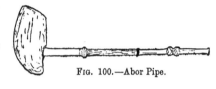

Fɪɢ. 100.—Abor Pipe.

These uncivilized hill tribes of the North-Eastern
and Eastern frontiers of Assam are a fierce fighting
stock, and are quite unlike the peoples of India

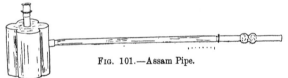

Fɪɢ. 101.—Assam Pipe.

proper.   Their everyday pipes are usually much
simpler than the specimens in Plate XII. and
Fig. 99. The Lushai pipe, Fig. 102,
is merely a thick section of bamboo,
which serves as a
bowl, with a slen-
der cane thrust into
it at right angles,

Fɪɢ. 102.—Lushai Pipe.

serving as stem and mouthpiece.   A simple geo-
metric ornament is incised round the bowl.   The

Lhota Nagas make a similar pipe, but some Naga
bowls are carved from wood, and have a conical
shape with the rim slightly higher in
front than at the back.   Two different
types are shown in Fig. 103 : the more

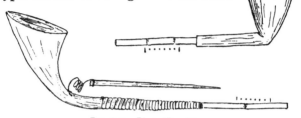

FIG. 103.—Lhota Naga Pipes.

elaborate one has a long, sharp thorn attached as
a pricker, and the stem is bound with split cane
tinted red.   These are prototypes of the chief's
pipe in Fig. 99.   Sometimes a
bamboo joint with a side shoot
is made use of for bowl and
stem respectively, as in the pipe   FIG. 104.—Sema Naga Pipe.
drawn in Fig. 104, which is a Sema Naga speci-
men.   These straight-stemmed plain pipes are

FIG. 105.—Mishmai Pipe.

called *tolupa*, but the
Nagas make also a water-
pipe, called *tsunküla* in
the Sema district, which
will be described later.   The Mishmai of the

Himalaya slopes use pipes of the same conical bowled type as the Nagas (Fig. 105), and since the cone shape lends itself to simple execution in metal, such metal pipes are not uncommon, a peculiar feature being a strut to bind bowl and stem, as seen in the example (Fig. 106) taken from the Dunhill collection.

It is remarkable that none of these pipes of Burmah or Assam are of the Chinese small-bowled

FIG. 106.—Mishmai Metal Pipe.

type, in spite of the fact that both the Karens and Shans trace their origin to China, while the Nagas, Mishmai, and Lushai occupy a region that has long been under cultural influences from the same source, since it is on a Chinese trade route. The Shans are a trading people, and Nyoungwe lies in the Ruby Mine area, so possibly the unique pottery bowls of this city were derivatives from patterns brought by early Portuguese or Moorish traders, while it would seem that the Karens and Nagas pipes are also based indirectly on European large-bowled models. It is interesting to notice the wide use of canes as pipe-material in tropical forest regions; the difficult problem of boring a stem and mouthpiece does not here present itself, as it does to people of cooler climates, where

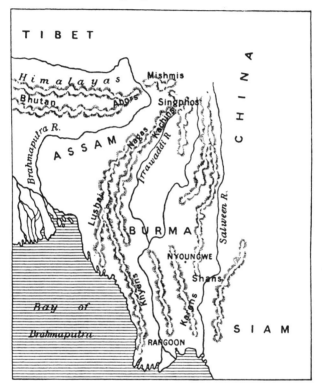

FIG. 107.—Sketch Map showing the Hill Tribes of N.E. India and Burmah.

the grasses and reeds are of too flimsy a character to be of much use.

A map (Fig. 107) showing the distribution of the hill-tribes mentioned has been inserted for reference.

The wild naked jungle tribes of the Malay peninsula are extravagantly fond of tobacco, but they smoke it in the form of a cigarette (*roko*), like the Malays from whom they have learned the habit, although they make use of bamboo for a tobacco-box, which is often beautifully decorated. A palm-leaf serves as a cigarette-paper, just as a maize husk was used by the Pima Indians, who used cigarettes, and not pipes, for ceremonial smoking. The pagan Malay tribes of the interior of Borneo—*e.g.*, the Kayans—are also great cigarette-smokers, using a banana leaf, which dries like paper, to roll the tobacco in, but they also make wooden pipes. In this case the pipes are derived from Chinese originals, since numerous Chinese pedlars go from village to village and are the chief links between these peoples and the outside world. A typical Kayan pipe is shown in Fig. 108, the stem being a section or sometimes a big internode of bamboo, resembling that of an opium pipe in its dimensions. Instead, however, of the elaborate porcelain bowl with its pin-point opening which is used by the Chinese opium-

smoker, the Borneo pipes have a tall, slender
hardwood bowl, not unlike that of a Chinese

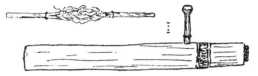

FIG. 108.—Kayan Pipe with Plug.

water-pipe. As in an opium pipe, the bowl is
usually, although not invariably, inserted at a considerable distance from the front end of the stem,
its position being normally dictated by the position
of the septum which separates the internodes.
A plug (shown in Fig. 108), formed of shavings or

FIG. 109.—Kayan Pipes of Natural Bamboo.

fibres packed into a cleft rattan, is inserted into the
stem to absorb the nicotine, and to prevent any ash
reaching the mouth. A bent bamboo, or a natural
root, sometimes suggests to the smoker some variant
upon the stock pattern, as for example in Fig. 109.
In Fig. 110 are shown Borneo opium pipes for

comparison : the Murut (slender-stemmed) example has a little brass bowl of Chinese type, into which a stone opium bowl has subsequently been fixed.

Pipes made in the Borneo style have passed from island to island, and are now in very extensive use

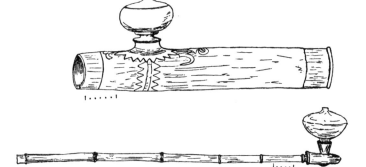

Fig. 110.—Opium Pipes of Borneo.

among the Papuans of New Guinea, a race distinct from the Malays. These people smoke in a very singular fashion. An individual takes the pipe and draws at it in the ordinary way until the big bamboo stem is full of smoke, when the open end is closed with the hand, the bowl removed, and the smoke inhaled through the nostrils from this orifice by each of the company in turn. The Dunhill collection contains some beautiful examples of

Papuan pipes (Plate XII.), some of which are elaborately decorated with conventional geometrical, floral, and animal designs. Instead of a hardwood bowl as used in Borneo, a simple length of cane is substituted, or even a twisted leaf, which can be renewed every time the pipe is used.

Short as is the distance between New Guinea and Australia by way of the Torres Straits, and even though the islanders of the Straits themselves used the Papuan pipe, the knowledge of tobacco did not pass into the southern continent until the days of Captain Cook. The Australian aborigines, ignorant of agriculture, with not even intelligence enough to gather the nuggets of gold that lay upon the ground, had nothing in the way of barter to offer to the Malay traders, who therefore avoided their coasts. Yet they were not without the solace of a narcotic, their substitute for tobacco being the leaves of the *Pitcheri* plant, which they gathered and chewed. The dried leaves are mixed with cassia or acacia-leaf ashes, and the "plug" when not in use is thrust by the black fellow into the tangled, greasy curls behind his ear, for being stark naked, he has no more convenient pocket. Since the *Pitcheri* plant grows only among the sandhills of the centre of Australia, it has been one of the

very few articles of inter-tribal trade among these
most primitive peoples. A decoction of the leaves
was also used to " doctor " a water pool known to be
frequented by emu, the bird becoming stupefied
after drinking, and thus falling an easy prey to the
hunters. In the nineteenth century, however,
a few Papuan pipes crossed the Straits, for Mr.
H. M. Moseley, the distinguished naturalist of the
Challenger Expedition, who visited this area in
1874, writes as follows; " The most prized
possession of these blacks (the Gudang tribe of
Cape Yorke) is, however, the bamboo pipe, of which
there were several in the camp. The bamboos are
procured by barter from the Murray Islanders, who
visit Cape Yorke from time to time, and the
tobacco is smoked in them by the Blacks in nearly
the same curious manner as that in vogue among
the Dalrymple Islanders. No doubt the Australians
have learned to smoke from the Murray Islanders.

" The tobacco pipe is a large joint of bamboo, as
much as two feet in length, and three inches in
diameter. There is a small round hole on the side at
one end, and a larger hole in the extremity of the
other end. A small cone of green leaf is inserted into
the smaller round hole and filled with tobacco, which
is lighted at the top as usual. A man, or oftener a

woman opening her mouth, covers the cone and lighted tobacco with it, thus having the leaf cone and burning tobacco entirely within her mouth. She then blows and forces the smoke into the cavity of the bamboo, keeping her hand over the hole at the other end, and closing this aperture as soon as the bamboo is full. The leaf cone is then withdrawn and the pipe handed to the smoker, who, putting his hand over the bottom hole to keep in the smoke, sucks at the hole in which the leaf was inserted, and uses his hand meanwhile as a valve to allow the requisite air to enter at the other end. The pipe being empty, the leaf is replaced and the process repeated. The smoke is thus inhaled quite cold." To put the lighted end of the tobacco in the mouth is not so unique a feat as might be supposed, for the negroes of Portuguese East Africa are described as habitually smoking their cigars in this fashion, while a similar salamander feat is reported from South America.

The Philippine Islands, lying not far to the north of Borneo, have a quite distinct series of pipe-shapes, which are extremely interesting. The Filipinos proper, who have been converted to Christianity and Europeanized by centuries of close contact with the Spanish conquerors, are

nearly always cigar-smokers, but the Igorrotes, who
are a somewhat primitive Malayan hill people of
the interior of Luzon, have a very elaborate art of
pipe-making. The patterns are those learned from
the Spaniards during the seventeenth century,
when the use of tobacco spread from Manila into
the interior with extraordinary rapidity, and hence
show Red Indian influence strongly, while in no
way resembling Chinese types. Here, as in
Paraguay, where it has been suggested that the
Spaniards introduced the pipe, a straight tube is
in common use; it may be carved from wood,

FIG. 111.—Pottery Tube
Pipe : Igorrotes.

modelled in clay, or welded in
metal. The example shown in
Fig. 111 is of clay, and has the
characteristic local ornament in
low relief. Besides the tube
pipes, pipes with bowls are made in great numbers,
those of pottery being grey, red, or black, according to the method of firing, and nearly always
having a band of ornament in relief in the angle
between the bowl and stem, which is slightly
obtuse. The metal bowls differ from the pottery
in having a " foot," and being at right angles to the
stem. They are first modelled in wax, from which
a clay mould is taken and fired, and this is filled

with metal; when the mould has been broken, the rough ornamentation of the metal bowl is picked out more sharply by means of a file. The journey-

FIG. 112.—Pottery Pipe with Characteristic Ornament.

man pipe-maker, who goes from village to village as he is required, can turn out only four bowls of the best type (which are those of brass) in the course of the day. Examples of clay and metal pipes are shown in Figs. 112, 113, and 114. It will be noticed that a straight cane stem and mouthpiece are

FIG. 113.—Pottery Bowl with Animal Figure.

inserted, as in the Paraguayan pipes. The actual bowls of the metal pipes resemble those of Burmah, but the stem in the latter is always curved. The pipe fashioned to represent a female figure (Fig. 115)

FIG. 114.—Metal Pipe : Igorrotes.

finds its parallel almost the world over. In very remote parts of the Philippines there are tribes

of yet more primitive character than the Igorrotes;
these are the almost Pygmy Negritos, among whom
arts and crafts are but little developed. They

FIG 115.—Bowl shaped as Female Figure.

have learnt to use tobacco, but simply
roll the leaf into a cigar. The cigar or
cheroot is also the favourite smoking
medium of the savage Malay race who
inhabit the mountains and forests of
Formosa, but these people make also a
crude pipe with a large, approximately
conical wooden bowl, into which a cane
stem is stuck at right angles (Fig. 116). An old
Spanish or Dutch model is probably the basis of
this type, which is certainly not Chinese or
Japanese. Some Formosa smokers
thrust a large cigar into the pipe bowl
instead of using cut tobacco.

Although they must
be classed as Far
Eastern pipes, the pipes
made and used by the

FIG. 116.—Formosan Pipe.

Battaks of Sumatra are in a category by themselves. They are entirely of brass, and those used
by persons of importance are of gigantic size,
although inferior folk must not presume to have
a very large pipe. Two specimens from the British

Museum are shown in Fig. 117. It will be noticed that they are of the large-bowled type, and very ornate in design, with long straight stems. It is possible that they have been developed from a pattern introduced into the Indies by the Portuguese in the sixteenth century, but it is difficult to imagine why an all-metal pipe should be made in a region where wood and cane are so abundant. The Battaks,

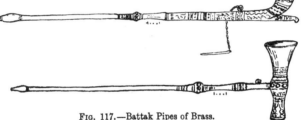

FIG. 117.—Battak Pipes of Brass.

however, are specially noted for their metal work, and, indeed, their whole level of material culture is unusually high. Living in a forested hill-country, and notorious for revolting cannibalistic practices, they were, until recently, able to maintain their independence, and to a large measure their isolation from the outside world, so that it is only to be expected that they should develop the art of pipe-making on lines peculiar to themselves. Since brass is costly, the very poorest among them are obliged to fall back upon a wooden bowl with bamboo stem, or they may compromise with a brass bowl and a cane stem (*e.g.*, the specimen in the Dunhill collection), but such a pipe would not be smoked by any Battak of good position. Also in the Dunhill collection (see Plate XII.) is a handsome pipe from Brunei, North Borneo, which in shape and general proportions resembles a Battak pipe, but the exquisite ornament, with its faithful rendering of gracefully disposed animals and plants, is the work of a Chinese craftsman, in comparison with whom the Battak is but a crude and clumsy barbarian.

FIG. 118.—Polynesian Shell Pipe.

It is interesting to find that the use of tobacco never spread from Malaysia to Polynesia, and it was left to Captain Cook and his successors to teach the peoples of the Pacific Ocean, including the New Zealanders, the art of smoking. Hence the pipes of this area are usually crude imitations of modern European patterns in shell, stone, or wood (see Figs. 118 and 119). Among certain of the islanders, however, notably the Marquesans, personal ornaments and objects of value are carved from the huge ivory tusk of the sperm whale or cachalot. A pipe-bowl of this material, ornamented with six carved human figures (Plate VII.) is included in the Dunhill collection, and is similar to one possessed by the late Mr. Bragge, which is now in the British Museum. The latter also contains a unique New Zealand pipe, formerly in the Christy collection (Fig. 120), in which the head of a weaving peg, carved to represent two tattooed Maoris, is adapted to form a bowl and mouthpiece. Another pipe (Fig. 121) is obviously modelled on an English briar, and has been fitted with an amber mouthpiece of English make, but it is carved in characteristic Maori fashion, the eye, formed of mother-of-pearl inlay, being repeated as an ornamental or probably significant *motif*, as in the case of the carvings by the tribes of North-West America.

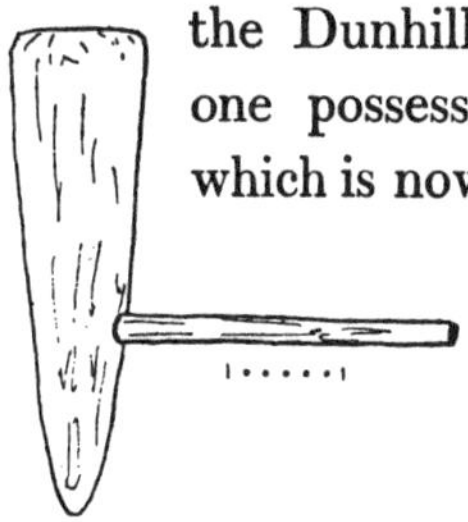

FIG. 119.—Stone Pipe : South Seas.

FIG. 120.—Unique Maori Pipe.

In the cannibal Solomon Islands (Buka and Bougainville) lying off New Guinea to the east, which were first visited by traders and missionaries in the early nineteenth century, there is a considerable native manufacture of pottery pipes modelled

on Dutch trade clays, and thus resembling the Kaffir pipes of South Africa. A British Museum specimen

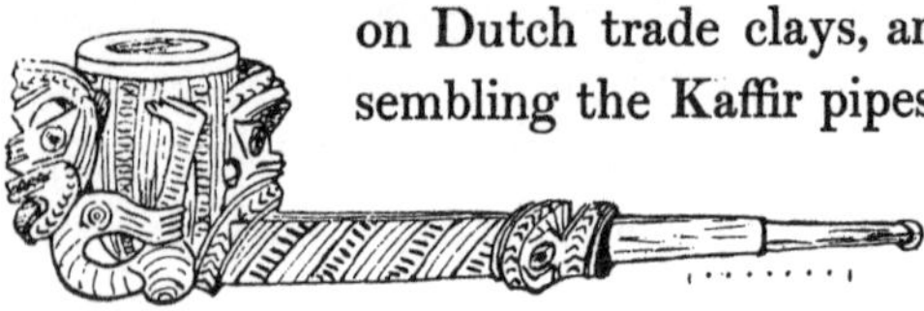

FIG. 121.—Maori Pipe : English Style.

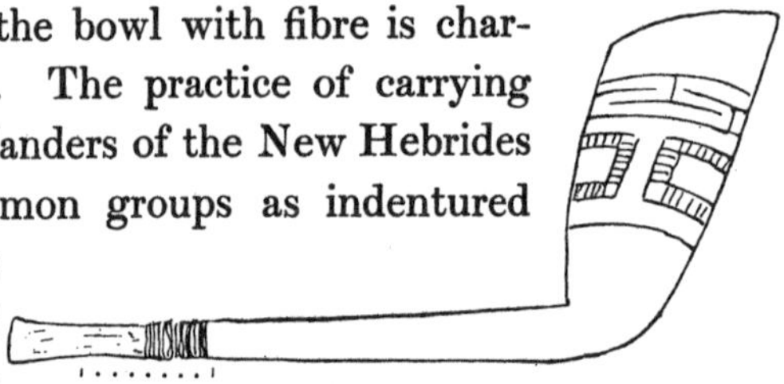

(Fig. 122) from this area, however, which is of black pottery, decorated with incised lines filled in with white, looks as if it had been copied from an English clay pattern. The binding of the wooden mouthpiece to the bowl with fibre is characteristic. The practice of carrying off the islanders of the New Hebrides and Solomon groups as indentured labourers into Fiji and other parts of

FIG. 122.—Solomon Islands Pipe : English Style.

the Pacific has, of course, led to a dissemination and mingling of arts and crafts, and this fact, coupled with the late introduction of smoking, makes the Pacific area of less interest to the pipe collector than would be expected.

CHAPTER IX

THE custom of cooling and cleansing the smoke of a tobacco pipe by drawing it through a vessel of water, is one that was never found in America, nor has it ever been customary among Europeans, yet it is almost universal in the East, and is practised also in Africa, where the unique dakka pipe is found. The existence of a method of smoking so distinct from that of the Europeans, who are supposed to have introduced the use of tobacco, is one of the facts that strengthen the case for the theory that smoking of some sort had a separate origin in the Old World, and antedates the *Discovery*. Indeed, as has been mentioned, Professor Weiner has gone so far as to suggest that both smoking and tobacco were carried to America from Africa some hundred years or so before Columbus. It has already been remarked that the Bushmen of South Africa use simple tube pipes, some of which resemble the implements found among Roman remains, while others are like the serpentine pipes of California. The Bushmen are now confined to the Kalahari Desert, but they were formerly much more widely distributed, and it is possible that the Pygmies who were known to the ancient Egyptians and to classical writers were their kinsfolk. Gradually, however, they have been driven from their hunting grounds by stronger peoples, and in South-West Africa they had been displaced by the Hottentots, a pastoral race, some time before the coming of the Dutch to the Cape, while in South-East Africa they had to give way to the Bantu peoples who crossed the Zambesi about the tenth century.

The Hottentots in their turn have been driven westward comparatively recently by the more powerful Bantus, who are at a higher stage of culture, and add the practice of agriculture to that of stock-breeding. As a result of these great racial movements, it would appear that the practice of the inhalation of hemp, dating from very early times, which was retained by the Bushmen, was brought south, and at some time took the form of pipe-smoking : from the Bushmen it passed first to the Hottentots, and later on to those tribes of Bantus with whom either Bushmen or Hottentots were most closely in contact. That it was not an original custom of the Bantus is suggested by the fact that it is far from being universal among them as it is among the Bushmen and Hottentots, and it was still spreading in the nineteenth century, for Livingstone remarks of the habit among the tribes of the Upper Zambesi that hemp-smoking was a vice of the younger generation, and was not practised by their elders.

As to how the transition was made among the Bushmen from the use of the simple tube or of the earth-pit pipe to the more elaborate dakka-pipe (so called from the native name for hemp), it is impossible to do more than surmise. It was probably found that by filling the mouth with water before inhaling the fumes of the hemp, the extreme violence and suddenness of its intoxicating effects was somewhat mitigated, for smoking through a mouthful of water as an individual practice is not uncommon. The next step was to insert the tube of the pipe into a vessel that could contain water, and such a vessel was not readily come by by the Bushmen, who have no manual arts. For ordinary purposes they carry water in the shell of an ostrich egg, but this is relatively fragile and awkward to handle; as a hunting people, however, they possess antelopes' horns which sometimes

serve as drinking vessels, and by making a hole
near the narrow end of the horn and inserting the
ordinary tube pipe, it was possible to "drink"
the dakka smoke through water. This necessitated
the stretching of the mouth completely over the
wide end of the horn, but this feat was not
difficult to a native, and, moreover, it ensured a
deep and thorough inhalation of the fumes, which
were drawn deeply into the lungs. A dakka pipe

FIG. 123.—Mountain Damara Dakka Pipe.

of the simple character described is shown in
Fig. 123, the particular specimen sketched belonging to a Mountain Damara, a people who, whatever
their ethnic affinities, are identical with the Bushmen
as regards culture. It was probably the practical
difficulty of getting a good fit as between bone and
stone that led to the commonest modification of
the dakka pipe, namely the mounting of the bowl
upon a cane stem which was inserted into the horn.
The spread of the custom also naturally introduced
variety into the patterns and the materials

employed; thus the tribes of Bechuanaland make
steatite bowls with a simple incised line ornament
which may be of the primitive
tube form (Fig. 124), but which
are more frequently of the
graceful vase shape shown in
Fig. 125. Among cattle-keeping peoples an ox-horn was frequently substituted for that of
an antelope, as in Fig. 126,

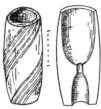

Fig. 124.—Bechuana Pipe
Bowl.

while the people of the moister regions north of

Fig. 125.—Bechu-
ana Pipe Bowl,
Vase Shape.

the Zambesi,
who commonly
made use of
gourd or bamboo
water-vessels,
introduced one
or other of these
into the construction of the
water pipe (Figs. 127 and
128). A further departure
from the original is made
when the gourd shape is
imitated in carved wood
(Fig. 129). Except in the
case of the bamboo pipe, all

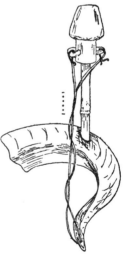

Fig. 126.—Kaffir Dakka Pipe.

these northern examples have an orifice of small dimensions, and no mouth-stretching is necessary. This is a modification always found where the pipe is to be used for ordinary smoking and not for deep inhalation, and in the Dunhill collection is an interesting example where the water-vessel is of ox-horn, with the wide end closed, and the mouthpiece at the narrow end. The use

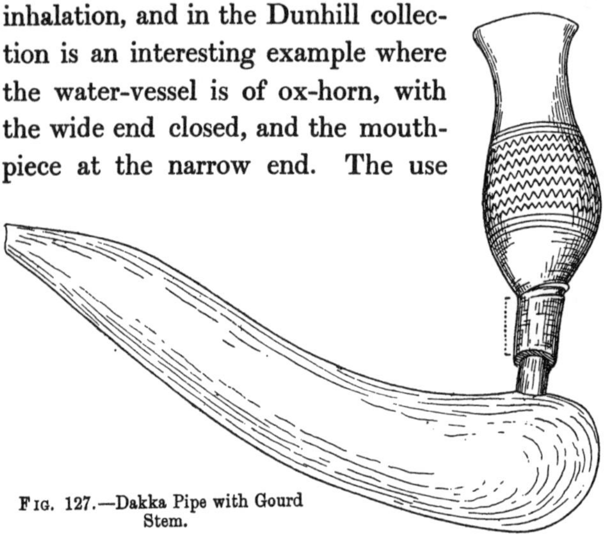

Fig. 127.—Dakka Pipe with Gourd Stem.

of a Stephen's ink bottle in this pipe, as a substitute for the usual stone bowl is an amusing instance of native ingenuity.

The stone bowls of the practically timberless region of the Kalahari, Bechuanaland, and the South-West generally, are replaced by wooden bowls in the well-timbered Zambesi Basin, where wood-working is a normal handicraft. Hence all the bowls of the pipes shown in Figs. 127, 128, 129, and 130, which come from Nyasaland, are carved from wood, and bear an elaborate geometrical

FIG. 128.—Dakka Pipe with Bamboo Stem.

ornament of incised lines, or of combined tooth and line, which is characteristic of the Savannah area. Three of the bowls are of a tall, slender, vase shape, and may perhaps be looked upon as developments of the tube-like bowl, while the one fitted to the stalked gourd (Fig. 130) is trumpet-shaped. The asymmetrical character of these bowls is noticeable.

Similar patterns are used in the ordinary tobacco-pipes of this region, which will be noticed in their place. Fig. 131 shows an enormous pipe, the water-vessel of twisted antelope horn, the bowl an unusual pattern carved

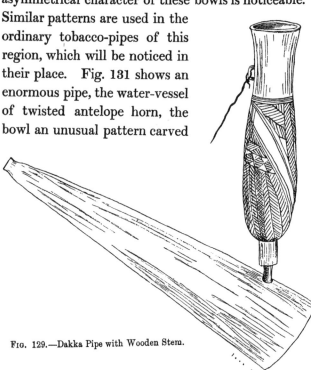

FIG. 129.—Dakka Pipe with Wooden Stem.

from black hardwood, the stem of ornamented cane, which came from the Lake Shirwa region in the Shiré Highlands. The side-loop for attaching the bowl to the water-vessel is a fairly constant and almost necessary feature in these awkwardly shaped pipes.

The Portuguese discoverers of the Cape route, although they stopped for wood and water in Table Bay, made no settlement there, and so it was not until the Dutch founded Cape Town in 1652 that close European contact with the South African native peoples (in the first instance the Hottentots) took place. The Dutch found dakka-smoking in full swing, although tobacco

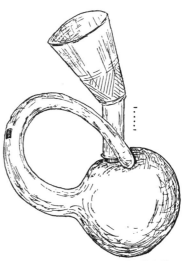

FIG. 130.—Gourd Pipe with Small Orifice.

immediately sprang into popularity and was either mixed with dakka or smoked alone, very often in a "trade" pipe. Kolben in his "History of the Hottentots" (1704) writes: "Dacha is a thing of which they are likewise mighty fond. It banishes care and anxiety, say they, like Wine or Brandy,

and inspires them with a million of delightful
fancies." He also describes how the constant
smoking of the women, with their babes either on
their back or at the breast, inures the tiny children
to the fumes of hemp or tobacco, and he declares

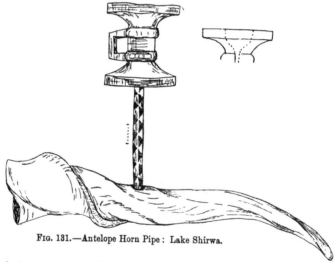

FIG. 131.—Antelope Horn Pipe : Lake Shirwa.

that a woman will put her pipe, when nearly out, to
the lips of a child just weaned, so that the smoking
habit is thus early acquired. Thunberg, writing
in 1772, says : " Both Caffres and Hottentots use a
pipe, either made of a long, slender and hollow
stick, with a hole near one end of it, in which is put
another hollow stick that is short, and has at the

top a cylindrical stone, which is hollowed out, and is the bowl that holds the tobacco ; or instead of the long stick an antelope's horn, viz., of the *capra onyx*, near the pointed end of which is bored a hole : in this is put a short hollow stick, and upon that the stone bowl. In smoking, they stretch their mouths over the wide end of the horn, and draw in a few large whiffs. The smoke they keep some time in their mouths, and then swallowing a part, puff the rest out again. The pipe then passes on to the next, and so goes round the whole circle. When strangers come to a Kraal or village, they are always treated with the tobacco pipe, which circulates in due form from one to the other."

The use of a " long, slender and hollow stick " instead of the usual horn is possibly to be explained as an attempt at imitating the long-stemmed Dutch pipe of the period.

The method of smoking dakka in a water pipe of the African natives must have been observed by the Arab slave-traders, who had a station as far south as Sofala, and during the sixteenth century, when they were in contact with the Portuguese, the Arabs grew to know, and to become inordin-ately fond of, tobacco. Hence, it is not fantastic to suppose that the Eastern water pipe, which was presently introduced into Persia and India, was the Arab adaptation of the dakka pipe to the new narcotic. The coco-nut palm grows along the East African coast, and the hollow nut, as a commonly used water-vessel, was substituted for the horn or gourd, while for convenience a long straight stem, serving as a mouthpiece, was added. This is the primitive form of the Indian *nargileh*, a word which means coco-nut, and although the modern patterns are made of metal and elaborately mounted, the shape and dimensions of the original coco - nut water - vessel can still be traced (Plate XIII.). In the Pitt-Rivers Museum at Oxford is a series of *nargilehs* showing the gradual evolution from the primitive to the elaborate form.

That the water pipe came into India in the earliest days of tobacco-smoking there, is evidenced by Sir Thomas Roe's description, written after his visit as Ambassador to the Mogul's Court in 1615. "Their way of taking it [*i.e.*, tobacco] is something odd and strange, tho' perhaps they don't fire their mouths by it as much as we do ; for they take a little narrow-necked Pot (that has an open round top, and a spout coming out of the Belly on't) and fill it with water up to the lower part of the Spout ; then they lay their tobacco loose in the top of the

Pot, and upon it a Coal of fire, and so with a Reed or Cane of an Ell long (which is inserted into the spout) they draw the Smoak into their mouths.

They say it is much more cool and wholesome to do it thus than as the Europeans do, since all the smoak falls upon the surface of the Water before it passes into the Cane. The Tobacco of this country is thought to be as good as any in the World." The pipe described by Sir Thomas was not the *nargileh*, but the Persian *kalian*, these people early substituting a modified type of one of the graceful vessels from which they poured water or wine for the crude coco-nut. The Persian water pipe sketched in Fig. 132, with its glazed and simply decorated pottery bowl, shows a decided affinity to the African dakka pipe through the *nargileh*.

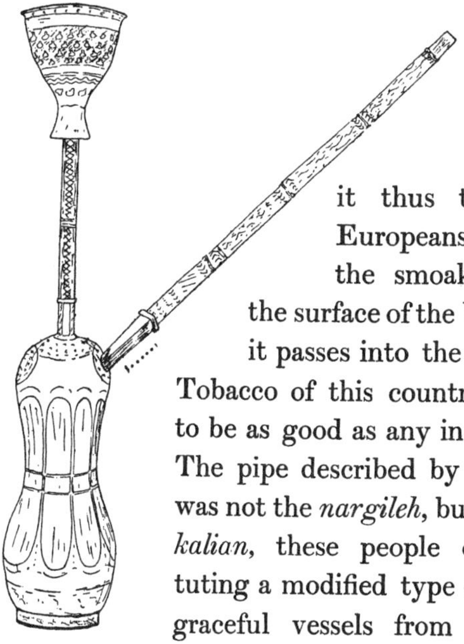

FIG. 132.—Persian Kalian.

The change in India from simpler to more

elaborate pipes may be traced in Indian art, as for example in the dated collection of Indian pictures in the British Museum (see Figs. 133 and 134).

FIG. 133.—The Nargileh in Indian Paintings (Eighteenth Century).

The insertion of the stem as well as the bowl in the mouth of the water vessel produced a more graceful outline, while the introduction of the long, flexible tube was a very necessary refinement when, as in the eighteenth century, ladies of leisure could hardly for a moment lay their pipes aside. Thus in one picture an artist shows a lady smoking while being washed by her maids, and in another she holds the mouthpiece

FIG. 134.—The Elaboration of the Nargileh.

still in her hand while with her lover's arm about her she gazes at a star-lit sky. A young girl pacing upon a terrace is followed by her maid, bearing the ever-ready *nargileh*, while a lover embracing his mistress upon a cushioned bed keeps one hand free to hold his pipe.

Persian smoking customs are interestingly described by the French traveller, Tavernier, who visited Turkey, Persia, and India in 1670. " The Persians," he writes, " both men and women, are so addicted to take tobacco, that to take tobacco from them is to take away their lives. So that if the King should prohibit tobacco for any time, he would lose a good part of his revenue. However, Shah Sefi in a humour having once forbidden tobacco to be taken in any part of his dominions, his Spies (that are in every city) found in the Indian Inn two rich merchants of that nation smoking their noses. Immediately they were seized and bound to be carried to the King, who commanded that they should pour molten lead down their throats till they were dead." This Shah Sefi was a grandson of Shah Abbas the Great, and reigned from 1628 to 1642 ; he was a weak and dissolute prince, and his commands, often issued in a fit of passion, were soon rescinded, so that smoking went on as before. Indeed his son, Shah Abbas II., who was no less cruel than his father, was himself a great smoker, and had the tongue of his pipe-bearer cut out for uttering a chance impatient word when summoned in haste.

The idle women of the harems took tobacco all day long, and the use of the water pipe, cooling and cleansing the smoke as it did, went far to make this possible without ill effects. Even among the poorer classes the custom had taken firm root, for, says Tavernier: " A poor Tradesman that has not above five halfpence to spend, will lay out three of them upon tobacco." Opium was at this time taken in the form of pills, and liquors made from poppy seed and hemp were drunk. Tavernier also notes that the Usbegs had brought into Persia the custom of smoking hemp in tobacco pipes. This is of interest, since the Usbegs are a steppe people who occupy the homeland of the ancient Scythians, reported by Herodotus to inhale hemp, while among them the presumably primitive practice of earth-smoking has to this day been preserved.

The Indian merchants and Arab traders naturally carried their water pipes to the East Indies, which was the principal zone of contact with the Chinese. The latter adopted the principle of the water pipe, since it was well adapted to an opium and tobacco mixture, but they developed it in a style peculiar to themselves. The hard-working Chinaman has not the leisure of the Easterners of more tropical lands, he does not sit cross-legged upon the ground, nor does he recline habitually upon a cushioned divan : hence the cumbersome and elaborate hookah or *kalian* is replaced in China by a water pipe that can be held in the hand, and that can be smoked while sitting upon a chair or walking. The pipe is made entirely of metal, and has an upright stem curving towards the mouth ; the tiny metal bowl is on top of a metal tube, which drops down into the water vessel. Two common patterns are shown in the centre of Plate XIV., two examples combining a tobacco-box with the pipe, and being fitted with two bowls, one for tobacco and one for opium. These pipes are often beautifully chased, or inlaid with enamel, as in the case of the Dunhill Museum specimens, also in this Plate.

The hill peoples of Indo-China and Assam, whose ordinary pipes have already been described, have in many cases adopted the Chinese type of water pipe, with modifications due to the materials at their disposal, to the limitations of their craftsmanship, and to the fact that their ordinary pipes are not of Chinese patterns, but have large bowls. In the case of the Kachin pipe (Fig. 135), the Chinese bowl has been imitated in carved wood, while the water vessel is also of wood, shaped like a nut, and the stem is of natural bamboo. The woman's water pipe in Fig. 136, which is that used by the Lakher tribes of Upper Burmah, has a large, vase-shaped clay bowl, a water vessel consisting of an upper part of carved wood, inserted into a detachable cane cup, and a straight cane stem.

The Sema Naga water pipe, or *tsumküla*,

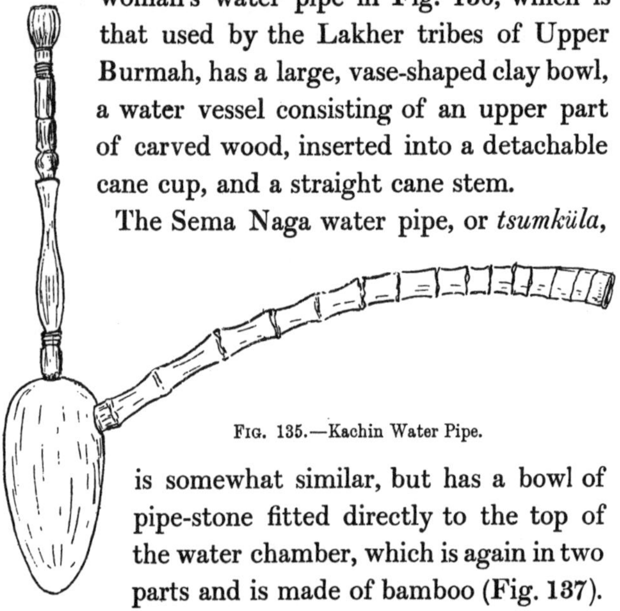

FIG. 135.—Kachin Water Pipe.

is somewhat similar, but has a bowl of pipe-stone fitted directly to the top of the water chamber, which is again in two parts and is made of bamboo (Fig. 137). The detachable water chamber serves an important purpose, for when the water is saturated with the oils and juices of the tobacco it is a favourite and powerful stimulant. Mr. Hutton, the leading authority on the Nagas, says: "The water of the chamber is considered fit to use after twenty-five or thirty pipes have been smoked, and the foul liquid then taken is put into a bamboo tube, in the cap of which is a small hole to let the noisome brew out drop by drop into the mouth of the user. This liquid, however, is not usually consumed, it is merely retained in the mouth and spat out again."

The Naga women, like the Lakhers, usually smoke only the water pipe, and it is their custom to bestow the precious, although deadly poisonous, pipe-liquor upon their lovers or husbands, or indeed upon anyone to whom they wish to show signal favour. Such attentions have often

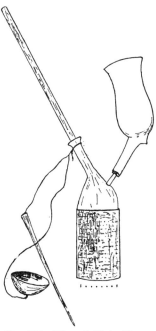

FIG. 136.—Woman's Water Pipe, Upper Burmah.

been an embarrassment to British military and civilian officers in Burmah, since it is difficult to refuse without offence so kindly intentioned a gift from a lady. It is said that the custom among women of almost incessant smoking is mainly due to the fact that the men depend upon them for this tobacco juice, which is considered invaluable during a fatiguing journey.

The water pipe or *nargileh* of the Arabs spread

not only eastward through Persia and India, but also westward through Asia Minor, Turkey, and North Africa, that is to say throughout the Mohammedan world. Here, however, it was in competition with pipes of European origin, which took the form

FIG. 137.—Sema Naga
Water Pipe.

of the *chibouque*, characterized by a large ornamental pottery bowl,

and a very long, straight stem. Such a stem, besides giving a very cool smoke, is adapted to the posture of the Turk, who sits cross-legged on the ground, and the pipe has spread into Georgia and Persia.

One of the earliest accounts of the *chibouque* is given us by William Lithgow, author of the "Rare Adventures," published in 1632. He was born in 1582, and as a young man of thirty travelled extensively in the East. While journeying be-

tween Aleppo and Damascus in 1612, he recalls
how the unusually pleasant and helpful demeanour
of his mule-driver alarmed him, as he thought it
concealed evil intentions. " But when I perceived
his extraordinary service and flattery was only to
have a share of the Tobacco I carried with me, I
freely bestowed a pound upon him, which he and
his fellows took as kindly as though it had been a
pound of Gold, for they are excessively addicted to
smoake, as Dutch men are to the Pot ; which ever
made me to carry Tobacco with me, to acquist their
favour, over and above their fials, more than ever I
did for my own use : for in those days I took none
at all, though now, as time altereth everything, I
am become a courtly Tobacconist ; more for fashion
than for liking. The Turkish Tobacco pipes are
more than a yard long and commonly of wood or
canes, being joined in three parts with lead or
white iron ; their severall mouths receiving at once
a whole ounce of Tobacco ; which lasteth a long
space, and because of the long pipes, the smoak is
exceedingly cold in their swallowing throats." The
reference to "severall mouths" seems to indicate
that these early Turkish pipes, or some of them,
had multiple bowls. Pipes with two and even
three bowls are not uncommon among the Kirghiz,

who probably learnt the use of tobacco from the Turks. A specimen now in the British Museum is sketched in Fig. 138. Other Kirghiz pipes show Russian and Central Asian influences, for these nomad people make many foreign contacts.

A typical *chibouque* from the Dunhill collection

FIG. 138.—Kirghiz Triple Pipe Bowl.

is shown in Plate XV. The bulbous mouthpiece, usually of amber, is a regular feature.

To return to the water pipe as found in Africa, it is fairly clear that the dakka pipe, which is the characteristic pipe of the Zambesi Basin and South Africa, has spread northward through Nyasaland and Tanganyika Territory, and north-westward into the inner margin of the Congo Basin. From Damaraland, too, it has spread through the Angola Highlands and by the coast trade-route to the Congo mouth, and thence comparatively recently up the Congo and its tributaries the Kasai and Ubanghi. The Arab penetration of Africa, especially inland from Zanzibar along the slave routes and southward

from Egypt by the Nile Valley, has also introduced
the *nargileh* into regions which probably had not been
reached by the dakka pipe.   Hence when modern
negro water pipes are examined, it is difficult to
decide whether they are
derived directly from the
dakka pipe, or indirectly
from it through the *nar-
gileh*, the more so as in
interior regions where the
coco-nut used for the *nargileh* is not found, it is
natural for the negroes to
substitute for it the bottle-
gourd which is in com-
mon use.   The specimen
in Fig. 139, which is from
the Nile-Congo watershed,
is obviously a direct copy
of a *nargileh*, while that in
Fig. 140 *a* from Nubia is

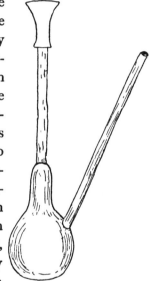

Fig. 139 —Water Pipe, Nile-
Congo Watershed.

also derived from the same model.   A   third
specimen (Fig. 140 *b*), of the type smoked by the
Baholoholo tribe living just to the west of Lake
Tanganyika, has the asymmetrical cone-shaped
bowl characteristic of Nyasaland to the south, but

the gourd has a long straight mouthpiece like a *nargileh*. The makers of this pipe smoke tobacco

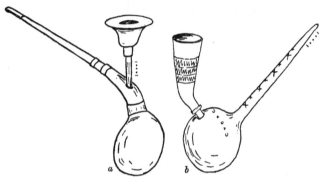

FIG. 140.—*a*, Water Pipe, Nubia; *b*, Water Pipe, Baholoholo Tribe.

and not hemp. For hemp-smoking the gourd

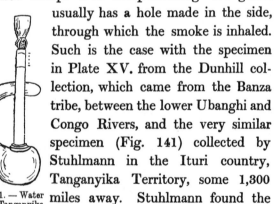

FIG. 141. — Water Pipe, Tanganyika Territory.

usually has a hole made in the side, through which the smoke is inhaled. Such is the case with the specimen in Plate XV. from the Dunhill collection, which came from the Banza tribe, between the lower Ubanghi and Congo Rivers, and the very similar specimen (Fig. 141) collected by Stuhlmann in the Ituri country, Tanganyika Territory, some 1,300 miles away. Stuhlmann found the cruder type shown in Fig. 142 in

general use among the Unyamwesi even in the
high plateau region round Tabora. In this case

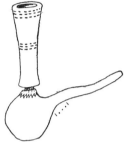

the clumsiness of the clay
bowl is due to it being made
by the owner of the pipe—
a man—pottery being nor-
mally a woman's craft in
this region. The Unyam-
wesi smoke both tobacco and
hemp, hence the long stem
of the gourd is used as a

FIG. 142.—Unyamwesi Water Pipe.

mouthpiece. A well-made water pipe of the
Wanyaturu tribe, also of
Tanganyika Territory, is
shown in Fig. 143. The
very interesting specimen
sketched in Fig. 144
is from the
Awemba tribe
of North-East-
ern Rhodesia
(west of Lake
Nyasa). It
should be com-

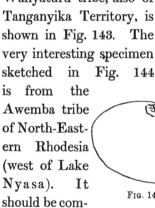
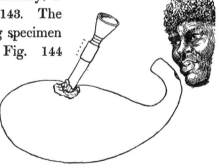

FIG. 143.—Wanyaturu Water Pipe.

pared with the Baholoholo pipe in Fig. 140. It
will be noticed that the stem of the gourd is wide-

mouthed, so that it is smoked after the manner of a horn dakka pipe, probably with hemp. It is decorated with native-drawn copper wire, which is stitched into the gourd before it is dried.

In the Western Congo and in Angola the bowl is very often inserted directly into the water vessel without any stem, as in the Mountain Damara pipe (Fig. 123), from which the pipes are probably derived. Some of the gourds

FIG. 144.—Awemba Water Pipe.

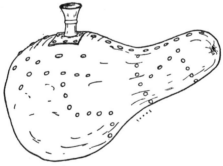

FIG. 145.—Brass-studded Gourd Pipe, Angola.

are of enormous dimensions: for example, that in

Fig. 145, which is a foot and a half long, with circumference in proportion. It is decorated with brass studs, a very favourite ornament in the locality. Even more picturesque is that in Fig. 146, covered with a design representing humorously drawn human and animal figures, together with

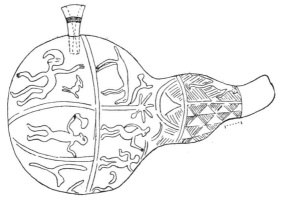

FIG. 146.—Huge Gourd Pipe, Angola.

an incised geometrical ornament. Both these are in the British Museum and come from the Loando tribe of Angola.

When Weissmann visited the Baluka tribe of the Congo in 1884-5, he found that their King had actually established a *riamba* or hemp-smoking cult in the place of fetish-worship, and enormous gourd pipes such as those sketched were being used.

Hemp was acclaimed as the universal saviour and helper, and as the holy symbol of peace and friendship, while the King's title of dignity was " Son of the Hemp." Yet to-day, not one in forty of the Baluka smoke hemp, nor is this to be wondered at, for the habit has such obvious and rapid evil effects, that a tribe adopting it universally for a generation or two would be destroyed. Hence the distribution of hemp-smoking in Africa is always changing, and is subject to no law ; there are tribes who are just giving it up, and tribes who are just taking to it:

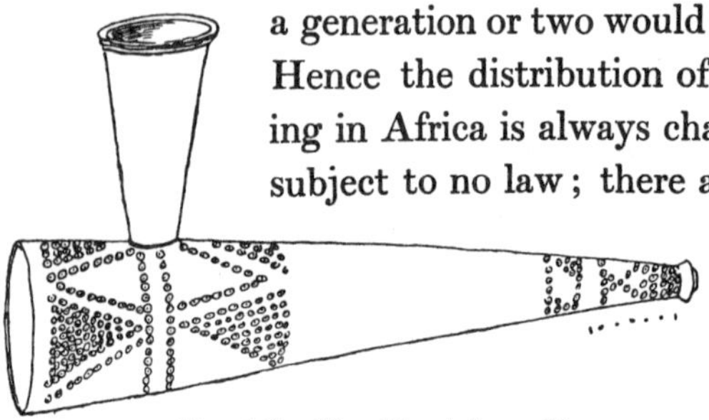

FIG. 147.—King Mtesa's Ivory Pipe.

tribes who look upon it with horror as criminal, living in close contact with tribes to whom it is a lawful indulgence.

One last water pipe merits description for its historical interest. It is a pipe of King Mtesa, the Waganda monarch who welcomed Speke to his Court, in the course of the latter's journey of discovery to the sources of the Nile. The pipe (Fig. 147) is carved from ivory, and doubtless the material used in part dictated the particular shape, but conical bowls are a common pattern in Uganda.

The stem resembles that carved from wood in imitation of a gourd, already sketched in Fig. 129. The use of ivory for personal ornaments and for warhorns is common in the Upper Nile and on the Nile-Congo watershed, where at one time a great trade in ivory was done. The circle and dot ornament, disposed in geometrical patterns, as seen on this pipe, is also characteristic of the native ivory-worker's art. It may owe something to Arab influence. As is so often the case with royal pipes, this is not the type smoked by the common folk of Uganda, nor, indeed, was it in general use at the Court. Speke relates how he would take out his meerschaum and smoke with the Dowager Queen, a stout, good-humoured dame, whose pipe had a clay bowl and a long stem like a Turkish *chibouque*.

Native Carving of a Gourd Smoker.

CHAPTER X

ALTHOUGH it is legitimate to suppose that hemp-smoking and the dakka pipe were indigenous to Africa, tobacco was almost certainly of European introduction, and, as everywhere else, sprang into immediate popularity. Indeed, the use of tobacco spread into the most remote corners of the Continent far in advance of the European trader or explorer, and hence the tobacco pipes of Africa show a variety and originality of pattern that is not to be met with in any other part of the globe.

The slave trade, so potent a factor for good and ill in the historical development of Africa, has played its part also in the history of smoking. The African native rarely leaves his home, he has no incentive to travel, and thus is strongly conservative in his habits. But the slave is a traveller by necessity, and he carries with him not only his own habits and customs, his skill in this or that craft, but very frequently also, as du Chaillu

162

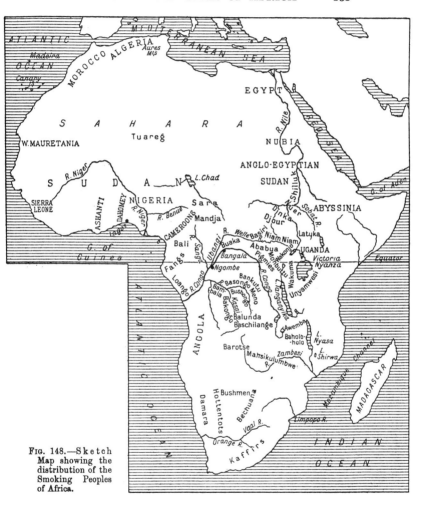

Fig. 148.—Sketch Map showing the distribution of the Smoking Peoples of Africa.

observed, makes shift to carry the seeds of the plants that grow in his garden at home, and by such means were pipes and tobacco disseminated.

The first and closest contact between the European and the Negro was established on the West Coast, where Portuguese trading stations came into existence before the discovery of America. The discovery of Brazil, made by the Portuguese themselves in 1500, was an accidental incident of a voyage directed towards the West Coast, and from that date Portuguese ships sailed constantly between the two regions, so that tobacco from the Brazilian plantations and pipes such as abound in Brazil were introduced to the region of the Gulf of Guinea very early in the sixteenth century. That century saw the establishment of the slave trade with the Indies, while the next brought the English, the French, and the Dutch also to the Coast. Here, then, there was an unexampled mingling of peoples—Europeans of many nations in contact with slaves and slave merchants from a hundred tribes of the interior. Not all the slaves were sold abroad—many were disposed of to native masters along the coast, many earned their freedom and returned to their homes, or made their escape. Hence there was constant coming and going, and it is little wonder that every collection of pipes will show a bewildering range of types from West Africa.

One of the earliest accounts of the negro smoker is to be found in Harris's " Travels," and is dated 1607 : " Tobacco is to them as much as half their livelihood.   And the Women are as violent Smoakers as the Men.   They press the Juice out of the Leaves when they are green and fresh, and then lay them a-drying on a sheard over the coals, and so cut them for Use : For they intimated by signs to us, that the Tobacco would make them drunk, if they took it with all its strength remaining in the Leaves.   The Bowls of their Pipes are made of Clay, and very large ; and in the lower end of them they stick a small hollow cane, a foot and a half long, through which they draw the Smoak : And this they are not contented to have only in their Mouths, but they must have it down their stomachs too, and so drink Tobacco in the strictest sense."   In Bosman's " Guinea," written at the end of the seventeenth century, we have a similar picture of the huge pipe (reminiscent of the Brazilian type as described by Nieuhoff) and the inordinate passion of the Negro for tobacco : " This country . . . produces . . . tobacco . . .

which stinks so abominably that it is impossible for anyone who is not very nice to continue near the Negroes when they smoke this devilish weed; which yet agrees very well with them.

"Some of them have pipes made of reeds which are about six foot long; to the end of which is fixed a stone or earthen bowl, so large that they can cram in two or three handfuls of tobacco; which pipe, thus filled, they without ceasing can easily smoke out; and they are not put to hold their pipe, for being so long it rests upon the ground. All the in-land Negroes take this tobacco, but those who live amongst us and daily converse with Europeans, have Portuguese, or rather Brazilian tobacco; which, though a little better, yet stinks to a great degree.

"Both the male and the female of the Negroes are so very fond of tobacco that they will part with the very last penny which should buy them bread, and suffer hunger rather than be without it; which so enhances the price, that for a Portuguese fathom, which is much less than one pound of this trash, they will give five shillings or a golden quarter of Jacobus.

"Let us therefore praise those smokers, my good friends, who take the noble Spanish or Virginian

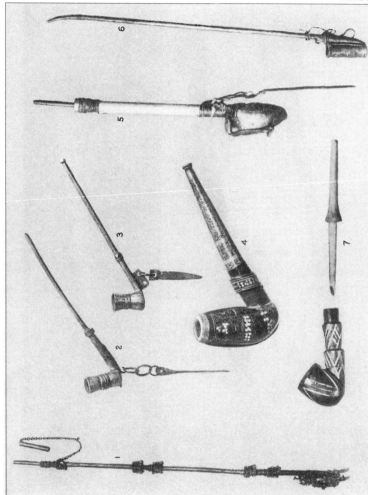

PLATE XX

5. NIGERIAN PIPE, LEATHER BOUND
6. CHIEF'S PIPE, NIGERIA
7. UGANDA PIPE

1. CHIEF'S PIPE, ASHANTI
2 and 3. TAUREG PIPES
4. A MOORISH PIPE

PLATE XXI

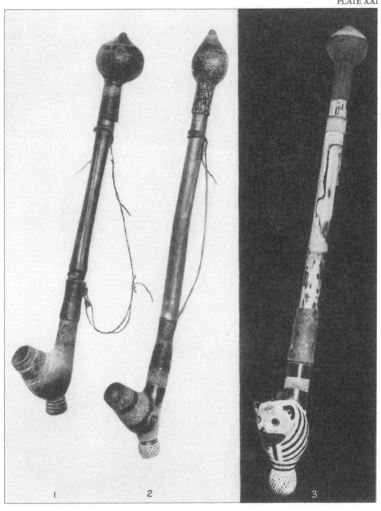

1 and 2. LATUKA PIPES, UPPER NILE
3. ORNAMENTAL NILOTIC PIPE

PLATE XXII

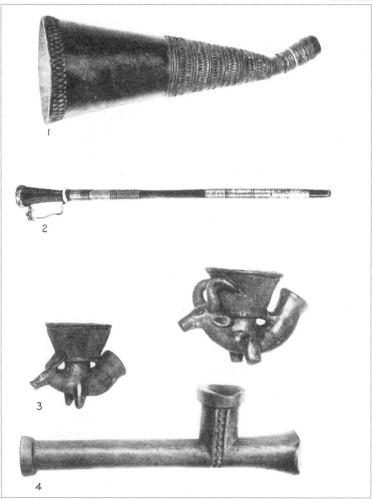

1. HUGE WOODEN PIPE BOWL
2. PIPE MOUNTED AS STAFF

3. MAHSIKULUMBWE PIPES
4. NYASALAND PIPE

PLATE XXIII

1. GERMAN PORCELAIN PIPE WITH ORNATE STEM
2. TYROLESE PIPE
3. BAVARIAN CARVED PIPE BOWL

PLATE XXIV

1. PORTRAIT OF NAPOLEON
2. FRENCH COMMEMORATIVE PIPE
3. FRENCH PORCELAIN PIPE

PLATE XXV

1. STAFFORDSHIRE BISCUIT-WARE PIPE 3. WHIELDON PIPE
2 & 5. STAFFORDSHIRE PIPES FROM THE WILLETT COLLECTION (*in Brighton Museum*)
4. STAFFORDSHIRE PIPE 6. COILED PIPE, POSSIBLY BY PRATT, 1780–1790

PLATE XXVI

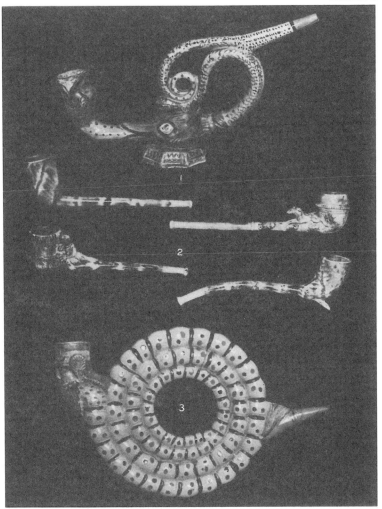

1 and 3. STAFFORDSHIRE-WARE PIPES
2. PIPES OF WHIELDON WARE

PLATE XXVII

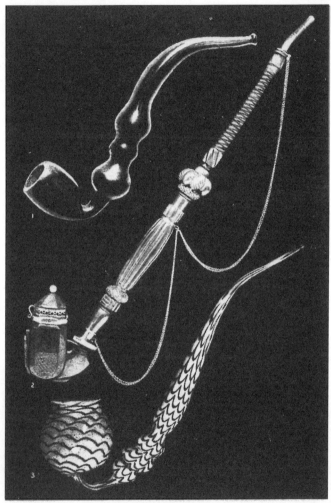

1 and 3. BRISTOL GLASS PIPES
2. VIENNESE AMBER PIPE

Tobacco; but as for those stupid wretches who content themselves with the Amorsfort weed, I heartily wish, as a punishment for their depraved taste, that during their life they may never smoke better than our Negroes, and Brazil [tobacco] on Sundays and holidays; yet under condition that they be obliged to keep company with each other, and be banished the company of genteel smokers." Amorsfort, Amersford, or Amesford, was a Dutch village near Deventer, where the first European plantation of tobacco was laid out in 1615. Perhaps it was his interest in West Indian trade that made Bosman, himself a Dutchman, so bitter against the use of the home-grown product.

Among native African pipes to-day, those of clay and of wood are about equally numerous, while metal pipes, although by no means rare, are less common, and are confined to a few localities. Even as between clay and wooden pipes, it is possible to distinguish parts of the Continent where either the one or the other will be the more popular.   Broadly speaking, it is in the huge primeval forest region, stretching from the Gulf of Guinea right across the Congo Basin to the Great Lakes, that the most elaborate and interesting varieties of wooden pipes are made, while in

the great crescent of grassy Savannahs which sur-
rounds the forests to the north, the east and the
south, pottery bowls, varying from crude makeshifts to beautifully finished specimens of graceful
design, take pride of place. Wooden pipes, it
would seem, are not well suited to the extremely
dry atmospheric conditions occurring for part of
each year in the grass-lands.

Although it appears that tobacco and the
tobacco pipe passed into Africa from the West
Coast, the actual form of the pipe must have
undergone wonderful transformations on its journey,
and it is not possible to trace out the evolution of
the innumerable pipes to be met with. Certainly
they have suffered no diminution of size, for the
Negro is gross in his appetites, and for him,
" bigger " is usually a synonym for " better." The
West Coast itself is, however, in this respect an
exception, for here, probably owing to constant
European influence, many dainty little pipe-bowls
are to be found. The question naturally arises:
When the tobacco habit passed westward into the
forest, and northward towards the Sahara, did any
pre-existing smoking custom prepare for it a
welcome ? This question has been answered in
the affirmative as regards South Africa, and the

dakka pipe was traced back to the simple tube through which hemp-smoke was inhaled. Now, just such a bone-tube pipe as has been found among the women of Bushman and Hottentot race, is in universal use among the Berbers of North Africa, except where they are in close contact with Europeans or Arabs. Fig. 149 shows such a

FIG. 149.—Berber Bone-tube Pipe and Pricker.

sheep-bone pipe, with an iron pricker for cleaning it, which forms part of the normal smoker's outfit (including also a flint and steel), contained in a decorated leather case and hung about the neck of every peasant in Western Mauretania. In the next figure (Fig. 150) is the European type of pipe, the decoration—*e.g.*, the fluted stem—showing Moorish influence, which is used by the wealthy in the same region. A similar simple bone pipe from the secluded Aurès

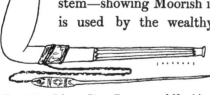

FIG. 150.—Saharan Pipe : European and Moorish Style.

mountain region in Algeria is shown at the Pitt-Rivers Museum, while many travellers in the interior of North Africa have described such pipes. The Red Indian bone-tube pipe, made from the metatarsal bone of the deer, as shown in Fig. 19, makes an interesting comparison. Now, a reliable tradition states that tobacco came to the Saharan region from the South—*i.e.*, from the Sudan— where, however, the pipes are of an entirely different type. Hence it is possible that in the Sahara, as in South Africa, an age-old practice of inhaling the fumes of hemp through a tube had persisted until superseded by the more healthy and hence more universal use of tobacco. No tube pipe is found on the Guinea Coast or in the Western Sudan itself, for throughout this region a stimulant was, and still is, in use in the shape of the locally grown Kola-nut, which is chewed, and not inhaled.

When the central forest region is examined, however, it is possible to come to the same conclusion as regards narcotics as in the case of the Sahara. In a recent careful study of the Ababua, a people living between the Welle and Aruwimi Rivers, in one of the least known parts of the Congo Basin, it was observed that they smoked hemp, finely divided and wrapped in a leaf, which was stuffed into a hollow tube made from the midrib of a plantain leaf. The same people smoke *tobacco* in wooden pipes resembling those of their neighbours. An exactly similar tube pipe (although used for tobacco) is described by a recent observer as made in the Pangwe country (see Fig. 151), the home of the Fang tribes, in the South Cameroons. Elsewhere rib-tube and leaf-cone pipes are common, although the influence of the introduced tobacco-pipe has led to the insertion of the cone at right angles to the stem (Fig. 2). Such was the pipe of

FIG. 151.—Tube Pipe: Fang Tribe.

the pygmy folk of the Ituri River, one of the small streams of the Aruwimi, and such was the pipe of the Monbuttu (or Mambutto), whose country lies between that of the Ituri pygmies and the Ababua. Stuhlmann, the companion of Emir Pasha, who examined many of the banana-leaf huts of the pygmies, found in them also a great many pipes in which, instead of the leaf-rib of a banana, a reed strengthened with a binding of bast formed the stem. The pygmies being forest hunters, and as such not always having access to a Negro banana plantation, such a substitute must often be necessary.

Among the Monbuttu, the natural curved form

of the primitive leaf-rib pipe has been stereotyped
in that of the more elaborate wood and metal pipes,
which all show the long, curving and tapering stem
This is strikingly shown in the huge chief's pipe,
over ten feet long, which is to be seen in the British
Museum (Fig. 152). This is made from wood (the
spatulate end faithfully imitating that of the leaf-
rib), and is bound from end to end with a ribbon
of copper. This material, which is beaten out of

FIG. 152.—Monbuttu Chief's Pipe (10 feet long).

copper supplied from Dafur, ranks among the
Monbuttu as does gold among Europeans, and
hence such a pipe represents an ostentatious display of wealth which would appeal to the un-
cultured mind. The two little legs on which this
pipe rests are typical of Monbuttu workmanship,
most of their wooden utensils—*e.g.*, small boxes—
being thus provided. Often instead of the sweetly
smoking leaf-cone which formed the primitive pipe-
bowl, a cone of sheet copper or brass is substituted
by the Monbuttu, and the same thing is done in
the case of the tube pipe (Fig. 151) already described as in use among the Fangs.

In the Dunhill collection (Plate XVI.) is another
fine example of a Monbuttu chief's pipe, in this
case with two little metal cone bowls. The
same collection contains several other pipes from
the north of the Congo Basin with the bowls of
this type. The concave, bow-like stem, so rare in
other parts of the world, is met with again and
again in the Congo region, and nowhere is it more
elaborately developed than among the Bushongo
and neighbouring peoples, who have been closely
studied by Messrs. Torday and Joyce. The pipes
of these savages are elaborately and often beautifully carved in symbolic patterns, and the set of
examples of the Congo pipe-makers' art which is
to be seen in the Dunhill collection is acknow-
ledged to be finer than that in the British Museum,
or indeed in any part of the world.

The Bushongo live in the south-central Congo,
between the Sunkeru and Kasai Rivers, their
neighbours to the west being the kindred Bakongo
and Bambala, who have similar pipes, as have the
Bakuba and Batetela, to the south and west. The
general characteristics common to all these pipes
are shown in the sketch in Fig. 153. Whether the
curvilinear stem is here due to a leaf-rib model is
open to question; it may, of course, be based on

the natural curve of a twig or shoot originally used
as a stem.   Certainly the Basongo Meno, who live
on the right bank of the Sunkeru, make use of a
different variety of " natural " pipe which might be

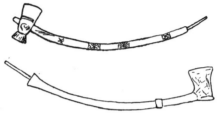

FIG. 153.—Bushongo Pipes.

the prototype of that of the Bushongo (Fig. 154).
Here a twig or shoot of suitable size is simply
bored through, the broader end serving as a bowl.
Were it not for the gourd mouthpiece, of which
more will be said later, this is simply the Ainu
pipe of North
Japan over again.

Interesting, be-
cause also so re-

FIG. 154.—Basongo Meno Pipe.

miniscent of Asia, is the Bankutu bamboo pipe
sketched in Fig. 155.   The Bankutu also live on
the right bank of the Sunkeru.

To return, however, to the carved Bushongo
pipes.   Whatever the design of the bowl, the part

of the latter adjoining the stem is sculptured in
high relief with an antelope (*Bambi*) head, often
highly conventionalized, so that it may be confused
with conventionalized representations of Mutu
Chembe (Head
of God), a deity
in the form of a
weevil, which is

FIG. 155.—Bankutu Pipe.

also a constant feature of Bushongo carvings.   The
pipe-bowls are often carved in the form of a human
head (see Plate XVI.), on which the tribal marks
are carefully shown, so that the pipes belonging
to members of different tribes are readily distinguished.   These tribal marks are raised scars,
formed by the method of cicatrization, which is the
form of body ornament here replacing tattooing.
Thus, three groups of these scars of elliptical shape
shows a Bambala man; three concentric circles on
each temple is the badge of a Bangongo; the
Isambo have tiny scars aligned in series of two,
three, or four, and so on.   The carving of the
Bushongo pipes is beautifully done, nor have the
figures the bestial hideousness which is characteristic of so much Negro work, especially in the
Cameroons and West Africa.

The curvilinear stem in an even more extreme

form is found among the people living on the
Ubanghi River. The characteristic pipe of the
Buaka is shown in Fig. 156. The stem, which is
covered with hide, is drawn round into a bow-

shape, while the vase-
like bowl is carved
from wood. The pipe
can be filled with
water and used for
hemp-smoking. In

FIG. 156.—Buaka Pipe.

the Dunhill collection is a specimen from the Basiri
tribe, who live further up the Ubanghi. This again
is covered with hide, and is heavily bound with

brass, after the fashion popular in this
region. Yet another Dunhill specimen comes from Ngombe, at the
Ubanghi-Congo junction. This pipe
is remarkable in that the stem is of
extremely fine plaited basket-work,
filled with red paste, so as to be
smoke- or water-tight (see Frontis-
piece). The art of basketry is highly
developed among many Negro tribes,

FIG. 157.—Mandja
Pipe.

and even drinking-cups of this material are known.

From much the same area as these bow-pipes,
although from different tribes, comes a singular

series resembling them as regards the bowl, but
having the stem straight, and inserted into the rind
of a heart-shaped fruit as big as a man's fist, which
serves as a mouthpiece.   This fruit rind may be
imitated in carved and polished wood.   Such is
the typical pipe of the Mandja people, who live
in the Basin of the Upper Shari (Fig. 157), while
the Dunhill collection contains three specimens
(Plate XVII.), including a very fine pipe of this
genus from the Welle River, which has the bowl
carved to represent a native head with tribal marks.
The fruit-rind, or its substitute, is stuffed with
grass or fibre, which serves as a trap to catch the
tobacco juices, and when saturated may be chewed.
The same function is fulfilled by the gourd which
forms the mouthpiece of the Basongo Meno pipe in
Fig. 154, and by the enlarged mouthpieces of the
two great wooden pipes shown in the Dunhill
collection, one from Basoko, the other from the
Kasai River (Plate XVII.).   The use of such a
filter becomes more frequent towards the north
and north-east, and is an almost universal feature
in the pipes of the Egyptian Sudan, presently to
be described.   Schweinfurth noticed it as characteristic of the Niam-Niam (Azundeh) pipes (Fig. 158)
of the Nile - Congo watershed, although he states

that these famous man-eating people did not chew
the unpleasant contents when they cleaned out

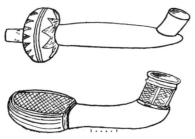

their pipes.   One
of the pipes which
he sketches has a
gourd filter, while
the other, although
the stem and bowl
are inserted differ-
ently, has an en-
larged mouthpiece

Fig. 158.—Niam-Niam Pipes.

reminiscent of the "fruit-rind" type.   This pipe,
however, like a very similar specimen in the British
Museum (Fig. 159), is made of pottery throughout,
so that the huge mouthpiece is not detachable and
cannot be stuffed with bast, or cleaned

out.   That these pipes are an imitation in pottery of the "fruit-rind"
pipe of neigh-
bouring tribes
seems con-
firmed by the
correspon-

Fig. 159.—Niam-Niam Pipe with Feet.

dence in the decoration of the mouthpiece between
the two, which is very noticeable on comparing the
specimens in Fig. 158 and Plate XVII. (3).

Often the wooden pipe-bowls of the form in Fig. 153 are bored right through to the bottom and then closed with a stopper, so that they can readily be cleaned when foul.

So far most of the pipes described have had stems perhaps a foot to two feet long, enabling the smoker to hold the bowl comfortably in his hand. If, however, the stem used is so very long, that when the smoker sits down the bowl rests upon

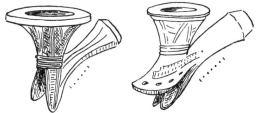

FIG. 160.—Pottery Bowls: Wavambo and Wakonjo.

the ground, a protuberance such as a foot, heel, or spur frequently appears, which keeps the pipe steady. Such adjuncts are most characteristic round the Guinea Gulf, where they are found also on the short-stemmed pipes, but they occur also a thousand miles away in the extreme east of the Congo Basin, near the Semiliki River. This is the home of the Wavambo, Wakonjo, and kindred tribes who were visited by Stuhlmann, and specimens of their black pottery bowls are sketched

in Fig. 160. Each bowl rests on two feet, and
the decoration consists of incised lines inlaid with
red pigment, after the fashion of the grass-land
neighbours of these tribes living still further east.
These bowls may be compared to that in Fig. 161,
which also has two flanges for the feet.   It is,

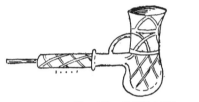

Fig. 161.—Bali Metal Pipe.

however, of metal, and is the work of the Bali
smiths of the Cameroons.   It shows a new feature,
in the shape of a finger loop, often a necessity for
Bali pipes, since they
are so large and heavy.
Another Bali metal
pipe, showing both
" feet " and loop, is
ingeniously developed

Fig. 162.—Bali Pipe with Elephant Motif.

from an elephant's
head pattern with multiple tusks (Fig. 162).   The
most striking Bali pipes are those carved from
wood, representing huge and hideous fetishes or

ancestral figures, such as appear over and over
again in West African domestic utensils and ornaments.   One such is shown in Fig. 163, while two
others from the Dunhill collection are
shown in Plate XVIII.   From the
same collection are three very remarkable pipes of large size, carved to
represent female figures (a favourite
subject with smokers of every land),

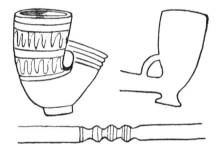

FIG. 163.—Bali
Fetish Pipe.   FIG. 164.—Bowls and Pipe Stem : Cameroons.

the first (Plate XIX.) from the Buaka country
(but showing Sudanese influence), the second from
the Baluba, the third from Loango.   Large black
pottery bowls are frequent in the Cameroons, some
plain, and some having (frequently in a rudimentary
form) the loop, the foot, or both (Fig. 164).
Cameroons pipe-stems are often carved in the

centre after the fashion shown in the same figure.

The pipes of the Coast peoples tend to show European influence as regards their shape and proportion, as for example the Lower Congo pipes sketched in Fig. 165. In the interior of Angola

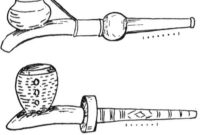

FIG. 165.—Lower Congo Pipes : One with Tribal Marks.

(Bihé Highlands) the mallet-shaped, clumsy wooden bowl already met with in the Congo is usual, and it is carved in one piece with the stem, which ends in a large wooden disc. The mouthpiece is a slender one, made of roughly welded iron, while brass bands and brass studs are

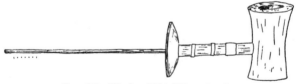

FIG. 166.—Wood and Metal Pipe : Angola.

favourite ornaments upon both bowl and stem (Fig. 166). The pottery pipe (Fig. 167) from the

northern Bambala people much further inland re-
peats the disc and the iron mouthpiece, although

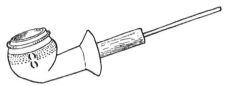

FIG. 167.—Bambala Pottery and Metal Pipe, with Tribal Marks.

the bowl and dimensions are rather suggestive of a
European pattern.   Both on this bowl and that in
Fig. 165 the tribal marks of the owner
or maker are shown.

Coming to the Guinea Coast, there
is a great variety of small black and
gray pottery bowls (Fig. 168), besides

FIG. 168.—Pottery
Bowl from Guinea
Coast.

brass bowls (Fig. 169), reminiscent of the famous
brass and bronze castings of the old city of Benin.

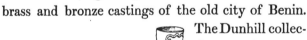

The Dunhill collec-
tion contains an un-
usually large brass

FIG. 169.—Brass Pipe from Guinea Coast.

pipe which be-
longed to a Dahomey chief (Plate XVIII.); like
so many chiefs' pipes, however, it is not typical of
the area, the general design being akin to that found
in the Sudan, while the decoration is Moorish in
character.   In Dahomey, where fetish worship pre-

vails, the human figure is often represented, as in the black pottery pipe (British Museum) in Fig. 170, which represents a man strangling a snake. Ex-

tremely interesting are the red pottery bowls, picked out in white, characteristic of Ashanti, for the various animals embodied in the designs (*e.g.*,

Fig. 170. — Pottery Pipe: Man and Snake, Dahomey.

wild cat, leopard, crocodile) are those which at one time had significance as totems, although there can hardly be said to be totem worship at the present day (Fig. 171). It should be remarked that on the Guinea Coast,

Fig. 171.—Ashanti Pipe Bowls : Vulture and Shell.

as in North America, the interest taken by Europeans in articles of native workmanship has led to their manufacture merely for sale as curios, so that many West African pipes are of this character, and may be of " freak " designs.

CHAPTER XI

THE MYRIAD PIPES OF AFRICA (*continued*)

PASSING from the forested Guinea Coast to the interior grass-lands of the Sudan, a region is reached where a higher type of culture, largely influenced by Mahommedanism, prevails. Fetishism, for example, disappears, and with it the constant representation of human figures in art, while cattle-rearing takes rank as an occupation of first importance, with leather-working as a resulting handicraft. The most constant features of Sudanese pipes are a tall and relatively slender bowl, and the setting of the bowl parallel to the stem, or at a very acute angle with it, so that the pipe hangs down from the lips like a Dutch pipe. In Nigeria, iron is favoured as a pipe material, for the smiths are very skilful, and a typical

FIG. 172. — Metal Pipe from Nigeria.

185

specimen, decked with leather tassels, is shown in
Fig. 172.   The iron prongs for supporting the bowl
on the ground are characteristic of the Western
Sudan only, and may be compared with the rests
already noticed on the bowls of the region just to
the south: they are, however, by no means a constant feature, and are absent in the chief's metal
pipe from Lokoja, Nigeria, shown in the Dunhill
collection (Plate XX.).   The rather elaborately
decorated metal pipe in Plate XX. (1), which is
provided with prongs, came from Ashanti, although
it is a Sudanese pattern.

The Kajoro, or tailed head-hunters of Nigeria,
add wooden feet to the long wooden pipes which
each smoker carves for himself, but they prefer to
use, if possible, metal pipes bought from the black-
smith, although to an outsider these seem far less
comfortable to smoke.   A specimen with a pottery
bowl from Rukabu in the Bauchi Plateau (Plate
XX. (5), Dunhill collection) has the bowl attached
to the stem, and also preserved from damage, by a
jacket of leather firmly stitched in place.   Such a
use of leather or hide in pipe-making becomes
increasingly common towards the Eastern Sudan.
Of great interest as an example of work of this
kind is the little pipe sketched in Fig. 173 (also

from the Dunhill collection), in which a polished
red pottery bowl (probably from the Mediterranean)
has been attached by a piece of fine kid-skin to one
of the little bone pipes
already mentioned as used
by the Berbers of the
Sahara. Fig. 174 shows
a typical Nigerian pottery
bowl, of the usual tall,

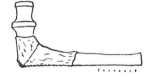

FIG. 173.—Pottery and Bone
Pipe: Leather Joint.

slender pattern, with a stem socket of snake-skin,
and the base bound with iron wire. Further examples from the same area of pottery vase-shaped
bowls are shown in Fig. 175.

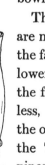

FIG. 174.—Ni-
geria Pottery
Bowl: Snake-
skin Socket.

The Tuareg, a noted desert people,
are not very great smokers, and, indeed,
the fact that the men habitually veil the
lower part of their faces would prevent
the formation of the habit. Neverthe-
less, their slaves cultivate tobacco in
the oases and smoke it, and some among
the Tuareg have dainty little metal
pipes, both portable and durable, of
which there are two specimens in the
Dunhill collection (Plate XX.). A
Moorish pipe, with typical ornament, is shown on
the same Plate. The fanatical Senussi are non-

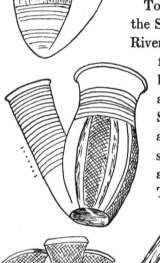

smokers from religious motives, but to the ordinary Mussulman smoking is an act indifferent, neither enjoined nor forbidden.

To the south of Lake Chad, the Saras, a tribe of the Shari River, make unusually graceful pottery pipes, the bowls in each case tall and slender, as in the Sudan, and lying at an acute angle with the stem. These patterns are shown in Fig. 176. The Mandjas, makers of the "fruit-rind" pipe already described (Fig. 157), are neighbours of the Saras to the south, and sometimes smoke similar pipes.

It is among the Nilotic people, however—the Shilluks,

FIG. 175.—Vase-shaped Pottery Bowls : Nigeria.

Dinkas, Nuers, Djours, and Latukas—that the most interesting, although not the most graceful, series of Sudanese pipes is to be found. The Nilotic

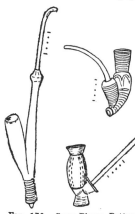

bowl is normally of clay, of the asymmetrical shape shown in Fig. 177, and, like the Nigerian bowls, is decorated with incised cross-hatching, as is so often the case also with Neolithic

FIG. 176.—Saras Pipes: Pottery Bowls.

pottery. It is fastened to the long wooden stem by means of a piece of hide which is put on wet, and shrinks tightly on drying. A pomegranate - shaped gourd, stuffed with bast, forms the mouth-piece, and this, too, may be attached to the

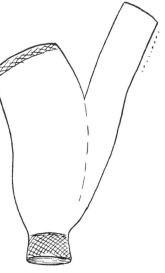

FIG. 177.—Typical Asymmetrical Nilotic Bowl.

stem by means of a strip of hide. The pipe is so

cumbersome that the smoker must be seated, and
a single pipe is passed from hand to hand round
the circle of friends. In
Fig. 178 is shown a Nuer
chief's pipe, forty inches
long, which was used in

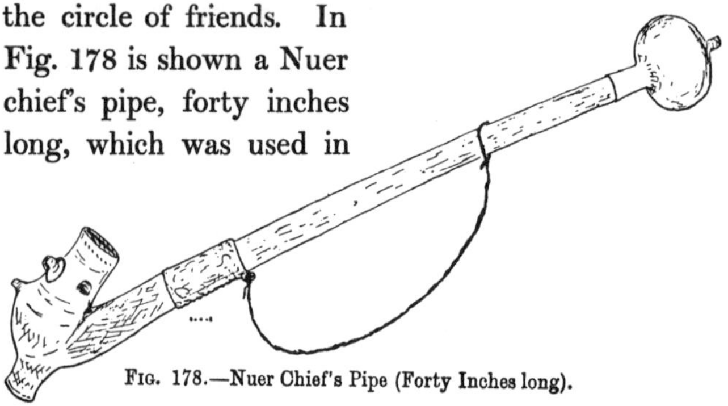

FIG. 178.—Nuer Chief's Pipe (Forty Inches long).

the council circle. This is a recent
addition to the British Museum.
The Dunhill collection has two
closely similar pipes from the
Latuka tribe, and an elaborately ornamented specimen
(Plate XXI. [3]), while yet
another specimen, formerly in
the Bragge collec-
tion, and brought
from the Sobat
River, is shown in
Fig. 179. Where

FIG. 179.—Sobat River and Dinka Pipes.

the bowl is of more elaborate pattern than usual, it

may rest in a socket of hide, as in the case of the Dinka pipe in the same figure, which has the entire stem of gourd: of the Nile Valley pipe in Fig. 180 *a*, which shows Egyptian influence in bowl, stem, and mouthpiece: and of the bowl in Fig. 180 *b*, which is shaped like a human head. All these are taken from drawings made for Mr. Bragge, as is also the slender-stemmed pipe,

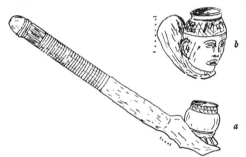

FIG. 180.—*a*, Nile Valley Pipe, showing Egyptian Influence ; *b*, Bowl shaped as Human Head : Hide Socket.

with carved wooden bowl no less than 10 inches high, shown in Fig. 181, which is merely marked by Bragge as coming from the White Nile, without reference to a particular tribe.

Further to the south, in Uganda, British East Africa, and Tanganyika Territory, a single, simple pipe form makes its appearance over and over again. It is characterized by a black conical

pottery bowl, and a long or short straight stem of
wood, or more rarely iron. In Fig. 182 is shown
the pattern used by the Unyamwesi,
the people of the highlands of the Tanganyika Territory, as an alternative to
the water pipe,
and in Fig. 183
the yet more
graceful type
made by the
Barundi, to the
north-east of

FIG. 181.—White Nile
Pipe.

Lake Tanganyika. The even simpler bowls
sketched in Fig. 184 *a* came from the
region to the west of Victoria Nyanza,
and many similar ones are shown in
the Dunhill collection, the example in
Plate XX. (7) showing an intelligent
anticipation of the inner tube device.
Sometimes the black pottery is decorated with incised lines inlaid alternately
with red and white pigment, as in the
larger example in Fig. 184 *b*. Here the

FIG. 182.—East
African Pot-
tery Pipe: Un-
yamwesi Tribe.

stem is at right angles to the bowl, a
feature which has become common possibly owing to European influence. It will be

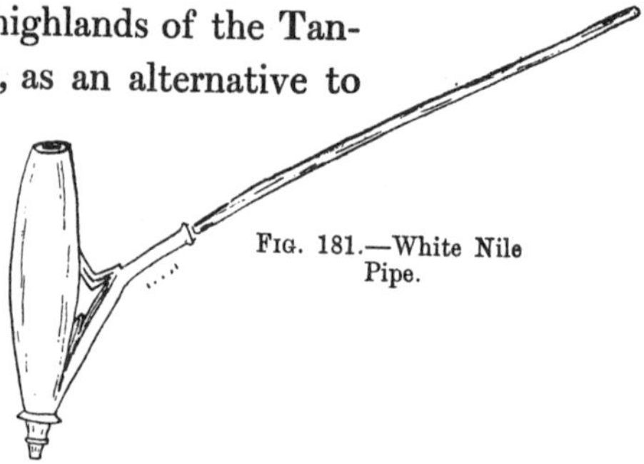

recalled that red and white decoration on black is
also employed by the Wakonjo and their kindred
on the forest margin just to the west
of the people under review. These
Wakonjo also make what must be
looked upon as the secondary pipe
shape of this whole region, namely,
one that has a round or cauldron-
shaped bowl, as in Fig. 185.   A fine
example of this type (the bowl about
1½ inches in diameter) was presented
by Sir Harry H. Johnston to the
British   Museum,   and   is   simply
labelled as from British East Africa
(Fig. 186).   As will be noticed, the stem is inserted
at the usual acute angle found in the cone-bowled

FIG. 183.—Pottery
Pipe : Barundi
Tribe.

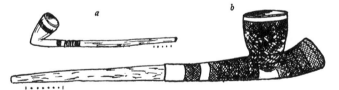

FIG. 184.—a, Pottery Pipe: Victoria Nyanza'; b, Pottery Pipe :
Incised Ornament, inlaid Red and White.

pipes. This pipe, which is of fine black pottery,
has a shadow-like decoration made up of finely
incised lines.   More usually the pipes show a very

delicate cross-hatching in incised lines, such a mode
of decoration being found throughout the African

grass-lands, and indeed among
most primitive potters, both
ancient and modern.

FIG. 185.—Cauldron-
shaped Bowl: East
Africa.

It should be mentioned that
not all the tribes in this part of

Africa are pipe-smokers, many of them, notably the
Masai, confining themselves almost entirely to
snuff-taking. Indeed, the native
snuff-boxes of Africa are so various
and interesting that they are worth
the collector's entire attention.

Mr. Roscoe, the anthropologist,

relates of the
Banjoro, a peo-
ple of North-
West Uganda,
that it is the
duty of a wife
to take charge
of her husband's

FIG. 186.—Pipe Collected by Sir Harry Johnston :
East Africa.

pipe, and have it ready for him when he comes in.
If a man wants to make trouble with his wife, and
yet can find no legitimate cause of complaint
against her, he puts his pipe where she is likely to

break it.   However careful she may be, the desired
accident happens at last, when the " aggrieved "
husband refuses the food she has prepared, and
goes off to sleep in another hut.   The wife turns in
despair to her mother for advice, and after a few
days her parents provide her with some beer, a
goat, and a new pipe, which the husband graciously
accepts, and so peace is restored.

Passing southwards through Tanganyika Territory, the dakka-pipe comes more and more into use
even for tobacco-smoking, and the large, asymmetrical, black, cone-shaped bowl, already described,
made usually of pottery, but sometimes of wood,
becomes the leading type.   Its size is sometimes
enormous, as in one of the specimens in the Dunhill
collection (Plate XXII.), which would easily hold
a pound of tobacco.   The same collection includes
a unique specimen mounted as a staff, which therefore falls into the category of a straight or " tube "
pipe (Plate XXII.).

A subsidiary pipe-form of this region, found
especially to the west of Lake Nyasa, is carved
from wood, the stem being very thick, and the
bowl nearly cylindrical, or slightly tapering, and
set at right angles to the stem, and a little way
back from the end (see Plate XXII).   In some cases

there are two bowls. In the case of the specimen shown in the plate, which is from the Dunhill collection, the stem is carved to imitate a human bone. This may point to a time in the past when a human bone was in actual fact in popular use as a pipe-stem (*cf.* the Chinese pipe referred to in Chapter II).

Passing inland to the Upper Zambesi Basin, an entirely new and unique pipe-form is found in common use, that of the Mahsikulumbwe, and

their neighbours and conquerors the Barotse (Plate XXII.). The pipe-bowl here is of black pottery, and is shaped like a basin, *i.e.*, is rather shallow for its diameter. It is decorated

Fig. 187.—Mahsikulumbwe Pipe : Antelope Supporter.

with the usual incised cross-hatching, very well executed, and rests on the back of an animal, whether some form of antelope, a buffalo, or a hippopotamus, of which only the head and forequarters are modelled, the two fore-legs, which are made short and thick, serving as rests for the pipe-bowl. The stem is, of course, long and inserted at such an angle as to allow the bowl to rest conveniently on the ground. A binding of copper wire is often used for ornament.

The example sketched in Fig. 187 shows clearly the method of conventionalizing the animal supporter's body so as to fulfil the requirements of a well-balanced bowl. The second example (Fig. 188) is a modification of the same design, and shows a different variety of antelope (the animal most frequently depicted). The third example (Fig. 189) is unusually elaborate, and is prob-

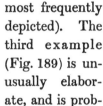

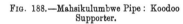

FIG. 188.—Mahsikulumbwe Pipe : Koodoo Supporter.

ably a chief's pipe : a lioness is carved above the bowl, with her fangs fixed in the forehead of a buffalo, which is here the supporting figure. This is from the British Museum collection, which includes also a pipe resting on a female

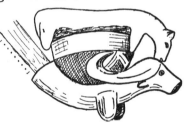

FIG. 189.—Mahsikulumbwe Pipe: Lioness and Buffalo Supporter.

hippopotamus, with her young one characteristically on her shoulders, and a specimen in which a bowed woman's figure supports the bowl. From the

Bakota tribe, also living in North-Eastern Rhodesia, comes the large red pottery bowl shown in Fig. 190.

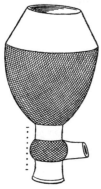

It has the characteristic line decoration, very beautifully executed in the original, but is based on the European bowl.

European-made, or more frequently European-pattern, pipes were introduced into the Cape region directly the Dutch made their settlement in 1652, and these rapidly put the native dakka-pipe into the second place. First the Hottentots, and then,

FIG. 190.—Red Pottery Bowl: Bakota Tribe.

as the Dutch spread inland, the Kaffirs, took to making pipes in the Dutch fashion, and nowadays fanciful variants of Dutch pipes, made in all sorts of materials, are characteristic of the whole of the Union of South Africa.

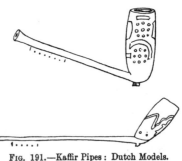

FIG. 191.—Kaffir Pipes: Dutch Models.

Fig. 191 shows imitations in wood inlaid with

metal, of ordinary Dutch trade "clays."   The example in Fig. 192, which is carved in one piece from serpentine, and has a finger-ring and a bone stem, is possibly based on a meerschaum.   Serpentine was a very favourite material with the Kaffirs, as it was also with the Red Indian pipe makers. Fig. 192 shows a pipe in this material with a thin

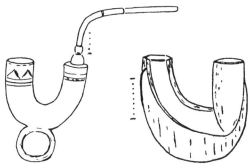

FIG. 192.—Kaffir Pipes of Serpentine.

flange beneath the bowl.   This is a copy of an old "trade" shape found also in North America, and is also imitated in wood.   The long, slender wooden pipe in Fig. 193 a is typically Dutch, and the same influence can be discerned in the numerous South African native pipes to be found in the Dunhill collection.   "Freak" pipes are also common, as for example the crude carvings of animals made by the Basutos, of which a specimen is shown in Fig. 193 *b*.

In a sense, Africa may be said to come to an end in the Sahara, for the Mediterranean shores form an area of which the arts and crafts were once those of

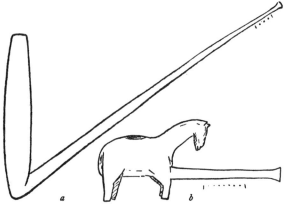

FIG. 193.—*a*, Wooden Kaffir Pipe : Dutch Model ; *b* Basuto Pipe of Carved Wood.

the Classical World, and were later identified with those of the conquering Arabs and Turks. Hence pottery and metal pipe-bowls of ornate design, smoked with long or short stems, or alternatively the *chibouque* or the hubble-bubble, are here in common use. Fig. 194 shows a typical Algerian bowl of wood, inlaid with metal, and set with semi-precious stones. The poor peasant, however, who cannot afford an elaborate bowl, can smoke a home-made pipe made after a fashion resembling Brazil. He hollows out a nut of vegetable ivory, which grows locally, and inserts a reed for a stem, producing the pipe shown in Fig. 195. It is in

FIG. 194.—Typical Algerian (Moorish) Pipe Bowl.

North Africa, too, that we meet the dainty little pipes for smoking *kaad*, a form of hemp or hashish,

FIG. 195.—Algerian Peasant Pipe: Bowl of Vegetable Ivory.

which, as regards their size and proportions, recall the pipes of Japan. A tiny pottery bowl, no bigger than an acorn-cup, and a reed stem, often prettily decorated in colour, suffices for the mere whiff of *kaad*, which is all that its dangerous properties make advisable. Such a miniature pipe may also be used by the desert wanderer, whose to- bacco is scanty, sup-

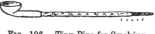

FIG. 196.—Tiny Pipe for Smoking *Kaad*.

posing his little bone tube to be wanting (see Fig. 196).

How precious tobacco is to the Arab nomad

is emphasized over and over again by Charles
Doughty in his famous " Arabia Deserta," and
although he speaks only of a region outside Africa,
his description of the Arab pipes and pipe-smoking
falls into place here. " As many Bedouin heads,
so many *galliuns* or tobacco pipes, with commonly
nothing to put in them. Is any man seen to have
any of the coveted leaf, knotted in his kerchief, he
durst not deny to divide it with them,—which if he
withheld, yet pretending mirth, the rest would
have it of him perforce. If there be none found
among them, they sit raking the old filth of their
galliuns and with sorry cheer put the coal upon
that, which they have mixed with a little powdered
dry camel-dung or some sere herbage : thus they
taste at least a savour (such sweetness to them) of
tobacco, whereof, when they are anywhile deprived,
I have seen them chop their pipe-stems small for
the little tobacco moisture which remained in
them : and laying a coal upon this drenched wood
they ' drink ' in the fume with a last solace.

" The best pipe-heads are those wrought in stone
by the hands of the Bedouins ; the better stone is
found two days below Héju and by Teyma.
Besides they use the *sebíl*, or earthenware bent
tube of the Syrian *haj* market. Their *galliun*

stem is made of the branch of some wild fig-tree, grown by desert waters, or of plum-tree from the oasis ; they bore it with a red-hot iron, over the evening watch-fires.   Comfortatives of the brain and vital spirits, and stay of importunate hunger, we find the Arabian nomads abandoned to the usage of coffee and tobacco ; in both they all observe the same customs and ceremony, which we might imagine therefore, without book, to be come down in their generations from some high antiquity.   So much are they idly given to these tent pleasures, that many Bedouins think they may hardly remember themselves of a morning, till they have sipped coffee, and ' drunk' upon it a *galliun* of tobacco."

CHAPTER XII

CLAY PIPES

THE typical English pipe until well within the last century was the "clay," and as plain clays have been manufactured for over four hundred years, there are so many varieties to be found that this one pipe-form may well engage the whole of a collector's attention. The chief interest lies in dating these pipes, and identifying the workshop from which they were turned out, and it is possible to attempt this since certain well-defined changes in shape and size took place from time to time, while makers' marks were frequently stamped upon the pipes, especially in the case of the earlier and more interesting examples. A great many marks have already been identified by searching the burgesses' Rolls of the localities where the pipes were found and comparing the names of citizens described as pipe-makers with the names and initials on the pipes. Collectors should refer to the articles upon Clay Tobacco Pipes in the

Archæological Journal for 1900 and 1901 by the late Mr. Hilton Price; to the volume on Ceramic Art of Great Britain by the late Llewellyn Jewitt; and to the pamphlets on the subject issued by the curators of the Hull and Belfast Municipal Museums respectively. There are also carefully dated collections of clays in the London Museum at Lancaster House (which includes Mr. Hilton Price's pipes), and in the Guildhall Museum, and material from all the sources mentioned has been drawn upon for the information which follows.

The first mention of English clay pipes dates back to the end of the sixteenth century, when Paul Hentzner, a foreign visitor to the Bear Garden at Southwark in 1598, says: " At these spectacles, and everywhere else, the English are constantly smoking tobacco and in this manner: They have pipes on purpose made of clay, into the further end of which they put the herb, so dry that it may be rubbed into powder, and putting fire to it they draw the smoke into their mouths, which they puff out again, through their nostrils, like funnels, along with it plenty of phlegm and defluxtion from the head." Clays are also probably referred to in the comment of William Camden, the contemporary historian, upon the return of the first unsuccessful colonists from Virginia in 1586. After declaring, mistakenly, as it would appear, that these Englishmen, led by Ralph Lane, were the *first* to bring tobacco into their country, having learnt its use (*contra cruditates*, says the Latin edition) from the Indians, he goes on to say : " In a short time many men, everywhere, some from wantonness, some for health sake, with an insatiable desire and greediness, sucked in the stinking smoke thereof, through an earthen pipe, which presently they blew out again through their nostrils, insomuch that tobacco shops are now as ordinary as taverns and tap-houses " (1615). It is interesting to notice from these references, and from contemporary woodcuts, that inhaling was regularly practised, so that the common phrase " to drink tobacco," used so often also by native peoples, was literally true. It is probable that some seeds of the tobacco plant were brought back from Virginia in 1586 by those who had learned to love smoking, for at about this time the cultivation of the plant was begun at Winchcombe, a little market-town in a fold of the Cotswolds, not far from Cheltenham. It was found a very profitable crop, and in spite of the prohibition of tobacco-growing in England, which was enacted in favour of the Virginian colonists, the Winchcombe farmers continued to grow it. Thus we read in " Pepys' Diary " (1667) : " She (his cousin) tells me how the life-guard, which we thought a little time since was sent down into the country about some insurrection, was sent to Winchcombe to spoil the tobacco there, which it seems the people there do plant contrary to law, and have always done, and still been under the danger of having it spoiled, as it hath been oftentimes, and yet they will continue to plant it."

When first introduced tobacco was exceedingly costly, since it was imported via Spain from the Spanish Colonies, the price being three shillings an ounce, or about eighteen shillings of our present money. Within fifty years it had cheapened to about eightpence an ounce, or four shillings of our money, for Virginia, which sent a first consignment in 1613, was producing half a million pounds by 1627. By 1675 or thereabouts, the widespread planting in both English and Spanish Colonies so glutted the market that growers obtained but two-pence a pound, while it was retailed at eightpence or tenpence, but in the reign of Queen Anne it was dearer again, and was purchased for one-and-eight a pound, the growers receiving about eleven pence.

As a result of the expense of smoking, the earliest clays were very tiny indeed, and it may generally be assumed that the smallest pipes in a collection can be put down as late Elizabethan.

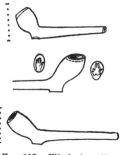

These are what are sometimes known as fairy pipes, elfin pipes, or Roman pipes, the latter because they were mistakenly attributed by some antiquarians to the Roman period. An excellent collection of such minute pipes is to be seen at the Guildhall Museum, their characteristic

Fig. 197.—Elizabethan Clays.

shape being shown in Fig. 197. The flat base or heel to the bowl, its barrel shape, and the way in which it leans forward, are all peculiarities of these very early pipes. The stems were probably twelve or more inches long, but unbroken specimens are very rare. In the London Museum is one, however, which is com-

Fig. 198.—Short-stemmed Clay.

plete (Fig. 198), possibly because the stem in this case is unusually short. On the other hand, this may be a cutty pipe or dhudeen of a century later. As a rule there was no decoration on these bowls, bu t occasionally an incised line or a milling was added. Unfortunately the makers' marks on these Elizabethan pipes of London make have not been identified. They include W. B., I. R., and S. (Fig. 199) on pipes at the London Museum (formerly in Mr. Hilton Price's collection), I. R. (several times), S., a hand, and a very imperfect leaf, at the Guildhall. In both museums there are many pipes besides of similar size and shape which are unstamped.

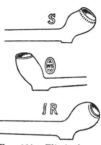

Fig. 199.—Elizabethan Clays with Makers' Marks.

Mr. Hilton Price has also described a pipe with a cup-shaped bowl and a very thick stem, having neither heel nor spur, but just pressed flat under-

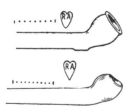

Fig. 200.—Sixteenth Century Clays.

neath to receive the maker's mark R. A. There is a very similar pipe to it, bearing the same mark, at the Guildhall, the colour being yellowish instead of white, while it has not the rim of the specimen described by Mr. Price, al-though, as it is imperfect, this may have been broken away (Fig. 200). Certainly it is the crudest

specimen in the collection, and this gives colour to
Mr. Price's suggestion that the R. A. pipes are
actually of the sixteenth century, and therefore
possibly those described by Hentzner in 1598. It
seems reasonable, indeed, to go farther, and to
suggest that Harrison, writing in 1573, had a pipe
of this type in his mind when he described " an
instrument formed like a little ladell " (see page 41),
for such a wording fits these particular clays very
well indeed. A somewhat similarly shaped pipe

from Broseley is figured by Jewitt
(Fig. 201), but no date is assigned to
it. It is claimed, however, that the
Broseley industry dates back to 1575,
and the " ladell " shape may have
originated there. The earliest draw-

FIG. 201.—Brose-
ley Clay: Arch-
aic Pattern.

ings of pipes are contained in the " Brevis Narratio "
of de Bry, an account of the Americas from contemporary sources published at Frankfurt-on-Main
in 1590. In the section devoted to the Indians of
Florida (based on Laudonnière's visit) an engraving
(Plate XX.) devoted to methods of curing the
sick shows a man smoking a very long-stemmed
pipe with a large clay or stone bowl (this is wrongly
described by Fairholt as a native of Brazil smoking);
while in the section on Virginia, based on the

English reports, an Indian is shown taking a meal, with a short one-piece pottery pipe 9-12 inches long on the ground beside him, of which a sketch is shown in Fig. 202. Carl Clusius, a Dutch botanist, who republished Monardes' "History of Medi-

FIG. 202.—Red Indian Pipe Figured by De Bry, 1590.

cine" in 1605, expressly states (quoting Hariot) that the English saw *clay* pipes in use among the Virginians, and brought some home for their own use in 1586, whereupon, owing to the rapid spread of smoking, especially among courtiers, a manufacture of similar clay pipes on a large scale was begun. Red Indian pottery and stone pipes which have been collected from the Atlantic Coast belt, and which probably resemble those seen by the first English visitors, are sketched in Figs. 17, 18, and 42, and should be compared with the clays. The Mexican red pottery pipe in Fig. 203 is post-Columbian, and suggests a very early European model, although it is much larger than a "clay."

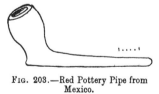

FIG. 203.—Red Pottery Pipe from Mexico.

It may be compared with the Cromwellian and later seventeenth century clays in Fig. 204. De Bry uses the Latin word "tubulum" for a pipe, but speaks of a more widely gaping part (*i.e.* the bowl)

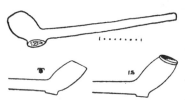

into which the tobacco was put, and a narrower part which was put in the mouth.

Coming on to the middle of the seven-

FIG. 204.—Cromwellian and Late Seventeenth Century Clays.

teenth century, we are on more certain ground in classifying clay pipes, for a number of makers put their full names on those they manufactured, and the date of their enrolment as burgesses has also been ascertained. Among these worthies are the Hunts of Bristol, a famous family of pipe-makers, whose marks, together with those of the Howells, are shown in Fig. 205. Sometimes the names were written in full: John, Flower, Jeffry or

FIG. 205.—Seventeenth Century Makers' Marks.

Thomas Hunt; and sometimes initials merely were used. A typical Hunt pipe is shown in Fig. 206: it has the rolling curves and marked "lean-over" of the earlier pipes, but is much larger, while the flat heel stands out in a more pronounced fashion from the stem. Contemporary pipe-makers were Philip Edwards, Humphrey Partridge, Thomas Smith, and Richard Nunney (Fig. 207), whose pipes differ in detail from those of the Hunts, but taken altogether give a good idea of what was typical of the period. The pipe

FIG. 206.—Typical Hunt Pipe.

by S. Wheticker in the Guildhall (Fig. 208) is probably of the same date (the fifth letter of the name is illegible, but C seems a possible interpolation).

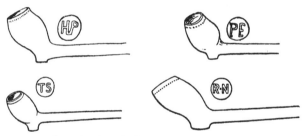

FIG. 207.—Pipes by Contemporaries of the Hunts.

Towards the end of the seventeenth century the tendency was to make the bowl with simpler curves and a less marked "lean-over," as in the case of the dated pipe (Fig. 209 a) of John Legg (1696), a Broseley maker, and probably son of the Richard Legg whose pipe-bowl figures in the Dunhill collection. A London Museum pipe dated about 1700 (marked S. H.) and showing

FIG. 208.—Mid-Seventeenth Century Pipe.

the new shape, is also sketched in Fig. 209 *b*. Of special interest in this connection are the two pipes of earlier and later date respectively

by Charles Riggs, of Newcastle - under - Lyme, sketched by Jewitt (Fig. 210), for these show not only an increasing size and change of shape, but the substitution of a "spur" for the flat heel, a modification which became more and more general as time went on, and which involved the placing of the maker's mark on the bowl (as in this

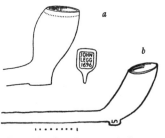

FIG. 209.—Late Seventeenth Century Pipes.

case) or on the stem, as in Fig. 211.

Some interesting notes upon pipe-clays, and upon the pipe-works of Charles Riggs occur in the writings of Dr. Plot, the county historian of the time of Charles II. Writing of Staffordshire in 1676, he says: "As for *Tobacco-pipe clays* they are found all over the country near Wrottesley House, and Stile Cop in Cannock Wood, whereof they make

pipes at Armitage and Lichfield, both which, though they are greyish clay, yet burn very white. There is tobacco-pipe clay also found at Darlaston, near Wednesbury; but of

FIG. 210.—Pipes by Charles Riggs: Appearance of Spur.

late dis-used, because of better and cheaper found in Monany-field, betwixt Wednesbury and Willingsworth, which is of a whitish colour, and makes excellent pipes, as doth also another of the same

FIG. 211.—Spurred Clay: Maker's Mark on Stem.

colour dug near the Salt Water poole in Pesnet Chase, about a mile and a half south of Dudley. And Charles Riggs,

of Newcastle, [*i.e.* Under-lyme] makes very good pipes of three sorts of clay—a white and blew—which he has from between Shelton and Hanley-Green, whereof the blew clay burns the whitest, but not so full as the white, *i.e.*, it shrinks more: but the best sort he has is from Grubber's Ash, being whitish mixt with yellow. It is a short brittle sort of clay, but burns full and white : yet he sometimes mixes it with the blew before mentioned."

The perishable nature of "clays" made the demand for them enormous, and the number of pipe-makers was correspondingly large. Mr. Sheppard, of the Hull Museum, quotes from the accounts of a country gentleman living in the reign of Queen Anne, and shows that he purchased something like a thousand pipes in the course of five years, an average of four a week. This would, however, include pipes brought out for the use of guests. The prices are interesting—three dozen of "best" pipes cost 11d., one groce (gross) of "Dutch" pipes 2s., and two groce of Nottingham pipes 5s. 6d., to which last was added 1s. 1d. for box and cord, and 8d. for carriage, making 8s. 3d. in all, which caused the purchaser to write in the margin of his account book: "Very dear, very dear."

The account books kept by Sarah Fell, the stepdaughter of the Quaker Charles Fox (1674-1677), show a much more modest expenditure upon pipes, such as befitted a Puritan household. There is an entry each year of " money paid for tobacco pipes on mother's account," the sums being 5d. (which included tobacco), 1d., 3d., and 1d. in the successive years. There are three entries relating to "Father," the purchases for him being "glue and tobacco pipes 3d.," "ink and tobacco pipes 8d.," "tobacco pipes" alone, 1d. On two occasions Mistress Fell bought a pennyworth of pipes "for my sister Susannah," and in 1677 there is an entry of a quarter of a pound of tobacco $2\frac{1}{2}$d., "for Sister Lower" (a married sister). Hence it appears that these Quaker ladies were smokers, albeit very moderate ones, the reason probably being that they held the view common at this period that the fumigatory effects of tobacco (*e.g.* against the plague) were valuable. It was used also, as these accounts show elsewhere, on the farm for curing sick animals, *e.g.* scabby sheep, and Pepys describes a coachman as curing his horse of the staggers by blowing tobacco smoke up its nostrils.

The woman pipe-smoker has never been absent in England, for not only did Jacobean ladies use their clays, but we read that the mysterious but respectable Mrs. Grace Poole, who kept hidden Mr. Rochester's lunatic wife, took a "moderate pipe" in the course of her daily visit to the kitchen. That Charlotte Brontë, the daughter of a remote

Yorkshire parsonage, wrote of this as of a matter exciting no comment, suggests that the habit was not unusual among serving-women of Georgian days.

The first pipe-maker in Hull has been identified as one Hugh Atkinson, who took up his freedom in 1664 (*i.e.*, when tobacco was cheapening), and from this man or his widow (who carried on the business after his death) are descended by successive apprenticeships all the Hull pipe-makers up to the middle of the eighteenth century. Indeed, when a Selby pipe-maker who married a Hull woman wished to set up in the town in 1683, the Corporation refused to make him a burgess on the ground that there were already more burgesses in that trade than could find employment. No fewer than sixteen pipe-makers voted at the election of 1724, but by 1774 the number had fallen to nine. Among them was a Robert Burrill, direct descendant of the man of the same name who was bound apprentice in 1676.

The eighteenth century brought a great variety of " fancy " clays, with the bowl moulded in relief, and in addition there was a rapid lengthening of the pipe stem, with the result of so increasing the likelihood of breakage that iron imitations were introduced, which, however, were too unpleasing in use to be a great success. Specimens are sketched in Fig. 212. In this connection, it is stated by Jewitt that a Broseley pipe-maker of the late eighteenth century, one Noah Roden, brought the long pipes to great perfection, supplying most of the London clubs and coffee-houses of his day. His family had been pipe-makers as far back as

FIG. 212.—Eighteenth Century Iron Pipes.

1681, and to the Rodens was due the introduction of " churchwardens " and " London straws," as the very long pipes were called. The Roden business was taken over by a Mr. Southorn, who received honourable mention for his pipes at the Exhibition of 1851. In 1868 he introduced steam power into his factory, and was then enabled to produce one and a half million pipes a year. The cheap briar and the cigarette, however, coupled with the expense of " boxing," have practically killed the demand for clays, and the manufacture at Broseley ceased a few years ago. The little shops in poor neighbourhoods, however, still have some sale for clays, the majority being marked with the name of

FIG. 213.—A Gauntlett Pipe.

" Crop " of London.

A pipe that deserves mention because of its interest to collectors, is the famous Gauntlett pipe, made by a man of that name at Winchester in the latter part of the seventeenth century, and stamped with a glove (see Fig. 213). These pipes are described by Aubrey the antiquarian, writing about 1680, but the Winchester pipes had long been noted, Ben Jonson, the friend of Shakespeare, declaring them to be the best that were made. The " Gauntlett " mark was frequently imitated, not only in England, but in Holland, so that not every pipe so marked is from this maker.

FIG. 214.—Thistle Head and Besom Pipe.

Fig. 214 *a* shows a " straight " clay fashioned like a thistle-head, and belonging to the late eighteenth or early nineteenth century (compare the French "besom" pipe in Fig. 214 *b*), while Fig. 215 shows a long-spurred, moulded pipe of the same period. Fig. 216 shows a clay pipe of 1924.

Although they lie outside the scope of this book, the bronze and other tobacco stoppers, often of graceful or fanciful design, and the large ember-tongs for lighting the

FIG. 215.—Late Eighteenth Century Moulded Pipe.

pipe before the days of the wax vesta, are objects which may well engage the attention of the collector of "clays," and the specimens to be seen in the London Museum and the Guildhall will serve as a guide in the first instance. Other "associated"

FIG. 216.—Clay Pipe of 1924.

objects are ornamented wooden cases for holding the shorter clays, stands for holding the long churchwardens, and iron holders (of which there is a specimen in the Dunhill collection) which were used for refiring the clays for the purpose of cleansing them. Fairholt says that the pipes of "parlour" customers were thus refired by the innkeeper for the use of those in the taproom.

The English pipe-makers were incorporated in 1619, the Dutch not until 1660, the headquarters of their industry being at Gouda, where tablets showing the five hundred odd Trade Marks granted

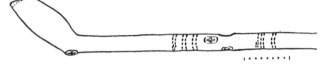

FIG. 217.—Old Dutch Clay, Seventeenth Century.

to makers from the inception of the Guild to the present day are preserved at the Guildhouse. Mr. Bragge had three of the earliest Dutch clay pipes *unbroken* in his collection, their measurements being $13\frac{1}{4}$, $13\frac{3}{4}$, and $17\frac{3}{4}$ inches respectively. These are now in the British Museum (although not on view) and are sketched in Figs. 217, 218, and 219.

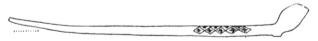

FIG. 218.—Old Dutch Clay, Late Seventeenth Century.

That in Fig. 217 has a very striking "lean-over," and the bowl is longer and more slender than that of the English pipes of the period (late seventeenth century). The stem is roughly milled and stamped with the *fleur de lys*, which is also the maker's mark. This design, which is found on the specimen in Fig. 217, and on many old Dutch pipes, is probably not the French emblem, but is a conventionalization of the tobacco plant. The second pipe, Fig. 218, with its more marked barrel bowl, is more like an English pipe, while in both cases the relatively long stem is curved slightly upwards,

FIG. 219.—Old Dutch Clay, Early Eighteenth Century.

and not downwards as in later pipes. The third specimen, Fig. 219, although it has a smaller bowl than the others, is of later date, for the convex curve on the inner side of the bowl has disappeared, while the flat heel has become very prominent, and is half-way towards its transformation to a spur. The stem is much less clumsy than in the earlier pipes, besides being several inches longer. The roughly incised lines around it indicate the point about which the pipe balances comfortably for smoking.

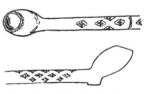

FIG. 220.—*Fleur de Lys* Pipes, Seventeenth Century.

Fig. 220 shows *fleur de lys* pipes of the seventeenth century from the London Museum and

Guildhall collections respectively, which may have
served as models for the Dutch pipes. Fig. 221
shows an eighteenth century Dutch trade clay.

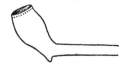

It is probable that whereas
the flat heel of the original
clays, with their comparatively
short, thick stems, was to en-
able them to stand upright

FIG. 221.—Dutch Trade Clay,
Eighteenth Century.

when laid aside, the lengthening of the heel, and its
transformation into a spur served the
important function of preventing the
head of the bowl from reaching the
table or other surface upon which it
might be rested during smoking or between whiffs. The clays made nowadays are of every imaginable pattern,
including exact imitations of briars, but
a large proportion of them still retain
the characteristic spur, even though,
in the case of a very short-stemmed pipe, it is
really useless.

FIG. 222.—Fancy
Clay, Eighteenth
Century.

CHAPTER XIII

SOME CHOICE EUROPEAN PIPES

In an oft-quoted passage from the writings of the gossip Aubrey, an antiquarian of the Restoration, referring to smoking it is stated : "In our part of North Wilts, Malmesbury Hundred, it came first into fashion by Sir Walter Long. They had first silver pipes, the ordinary sort made use of a walnut shell and a straw." Aubrey, however, was notoriously inaccurate, and as he is speaking of something that took place thirty or more years before he was born, there is no reason to suppose that the first Wiltshire smokers were unacquainted with " clays." In Elizabethan times, however, clays must have been difficult to procure in many out-of-the-way country districts, and no doubt all sorts of makeshift pipes, including the walnut-shell, would have been seen from time to time in use. It is also true that the clays were early imitated in silver, especially for presentation purposes, as contemporary records show, but there is no need to build upon this passage, as earlier writers have done, a theory that the earliest English pipes were usually of the character Aubrey describes.

Bragge had in his collection a little case of clays which tradition associated with Sir Walter Ralegh, and certainly since Sir Walter was for nearly fifty years of his life a smoker, he must have possessed many pipes during his lifetime. The case is inscribed in Latin : " It has been my companion in this most unhappy time," and such a tribute Ralegh might certainly have paid to that carved wooden pipe from Virginia which tradition says was his solace upon the scaffold in 1619. It is little wonder that the pipe, which had " come to court " as the companion of the courtly and popular Ralegh of the seventies and eighties, should suffer eclipse when the former favourite of Elizabeth lingered in the Tower a disgraced and seemingly dishonoured man. The dour and narrow-minded Scotsman, King James I., hated both Ralegh and the pipe, and issued his " Counterblaste " in the first year of his reign. " What honour or policie can move us to imitate the barbarous and beastly maners of the wilde, godlesse, and slavish Indians, especially in so vile and stinking a custom ? . . ." And following the royal example, the contemporary pamphleteer and poet, Joshua Sylvester, launched upon the smoking world a poem rich in violent invective entitled: "Tobacco Battered, and the Pipes Shattered (about their ears that idlely Idolize so base and barbarous a Weed; or at least-wise over-love so loathsome Vanity) by a Volley of Holy Shot Thundered from Mount Helicon." The dedication is to the Earl of Buckingham, Master of the King's Horse, who presumably was himself no smoker, and so found no offence in Sylvester's diatribes.

The metaphor of a gun-fire attack is maintained throughout this effusion, and Tobacco is destroyed in three "puffs," the whole "action" occupying some four hundred rhyming couplets. After making clear (as a concession to the Deity as Creator) that it is the abuse and not the legitimate use of tobacco that is his theme, Sylvester goes on to liken the pipe to a gun:

> "*Two smoakie Engines*, in this later age
> (*Satans* short circuit; the more sharp his rage),
> Have been invented by too-wanted Wit,
> Or rather vented forth from the *Infernal Pit*,
> GUNS and TOBACCO-PIPES, with *Fire* and *Smoak*,
> (At least) a Third part of Mankind to choak:
> (Which, happily th' Apocalypse foretold)
> Yet of the two, we may, think I, be bold,

> In some respects to think the Last, the Worst,
> (However Both in their Effects accurst.)
> For, Guns shoot *from-ward*, only at their Foen,
> Tobacco-Pipes, homeward, into their Owne
> (When, for the Touch-hole, firing the wrong end,
> Into our Selves the Poysons force in send)."

A little later on the natural association of ideas brings tobacco and hell together in the poet's mind, and he envisages the smoker in the fiery pit:

> "Then, in Despite, whoever dare say Nay,
> TOBACCONISTS, keep on your course: You may,
> If you continue in your *Smoakey* Use,
> The better for Hell's sulphury *Smoak* endure;
> And herein (as in all your other evill)
> Grow nearer still and liker to the Divell.
>
>   *   *   *   *   *
>
> It were the fittest Furniture (that may)
> For Devill, in a Picture or a play,
> To represent him with a Fiery Face,
> His Mouth and Nostrils puffing *Smoak* apace,
> With staring eyes, and in his griezely gripe,
> An over-grown, great, long TOBACCO-*PIPE*.
> Which sure (mee thinks) the most TOBACCONIST
> Must needs approve, and even applaud the Jest;
> But much more *Christians* hence observe, how evill
> It then becomes, that so becomes the Divell."

The use of the word Tobacconist for a smoker, and not as to-day for a seller of the herb, was usual at this period, and will be recalled as occurring in the passage quoted from William Lithgow (p. 153): " for in those days (1612) I took none at all, though now (1632), as time altereth everything, I am become a courtly tobacconist." The change in the attitude of those in high places towards tobacco which is hinted at here, was, of course, not unconnected with the fact that from being an import from foreign parts, as when Sylvester wrote, the leaf became, as already mentioned, the staple export of the English Colonies. It is Sylvester's references to the source of tobacco that fix the approximate date of his poem as 1614. Thus he writes :

> " For, Don Tobacco hath an ampler Raign
> Than Don Philippo, the Great King of Spain,
> In whose Dominions, for the most it growes."

while in another passage he refers to tobacco as coming from " Iberian Baalists," and to the " Iberian Argonauts," who by bringing tobacco to Europe had done more harm than by their persecutions and massacres in the Inquisition.   No insult is too great for this " poet " to hurl at the unfortunate tobacconist, and after comparing tobacco to hemp, since both have strangling properties, he continues with obvious relish :

> " And th' one prepareth Work unto the Tother.
>   For there do meet (I mean at Gail and Gallowes)
>   More of these beastly, base Tobacco-fellowes,
>   Than else to any profane haunt do use
>   (Excepting still the Play-house and the Stewes)
>   Sith 'tis their common lot (so double-choaked)
>   Just bacon like to be hanged up and smoaked :
>   A destiny as proper to befall
>   To moral Swine, as to swine naturall."

After which the likening of a smoker to a red-herring and a smoked sprat comes quite as an anti-climax.

It is interesting to find that just as a smoker is a tobacconist, or where the exigencies of rhyme demand it, a tobacconer, so the art of smoking is here termed tobacconing.

> " And for our Vulgar, by whose bold Abuse
>   Tobacconing hath got so general Use ;
>   How mightily have they since multiplied
>   Taverns, Tap-houses !"

There are many other references to the hold tobacco has taken upon the multitude, and that not of Englishmen only, but of foreigners :

> " But out it rushes, over-runs the whole,
>   And reaches well-ny round from Pole to Pole ;
>   Among the Moors, Turks, Tartars, Persians,
>   And other Ethnicks, (full of Ignorance). "

Yet on Sylvester's own showing, the amount of tobacco imported could only have provided for smokers in their tens of thousands, and certainly not in their millions. For turning his attack upon the merchants he says:

> " Let the Smoak-seller suffocate with Smoak:
>   Which, our Smoak-Merchants would no lesse befit;
>   TOBACCO-Mungers, bringers in of it
>   Which yerely costs (they say, by Audit found)
>   Of better Wares an hundred thousand pound."

As the price of tobacco must still have been a sovereign a pound or more, the import and consumption must have been trifling compared with that of to-day, when it averages 3 lbs. per head of population per annum. Taking the population of England when Sylvester wrote as about five millions, and the money spent on tobacco as a hundred thousand pounds, no more than 3 ozs. a head was available for them!

French and English smokers, as already related, brought the custom into Holland before 1600, and thence it travelled up the Rhine, but it was the soldiers who fought in the Thirty Years War of 1616-48 who carried pipes and tobacco throughout the length and breadth of Europe.

The typical Central European pipe of to-day

can be traced to the eighteenth-century Dutch clay. The porcelain bowl at its simplest (Fig. 223)

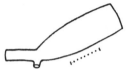

FIG. 223.—Central European Porcelain Bowl.

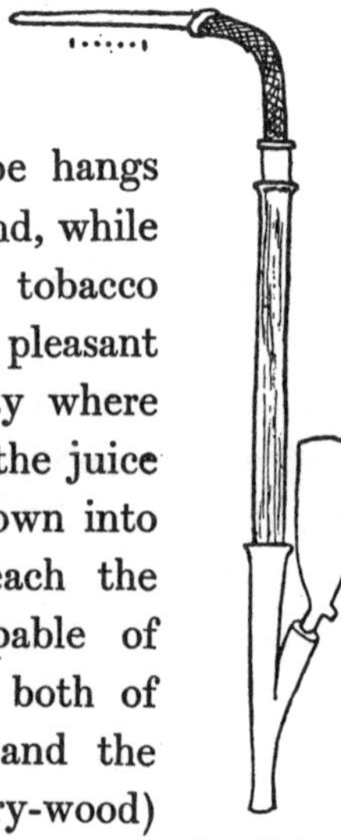

shows all the characteristics, including curves, proportions, lean-over, and spur, of its humbler model, although carried out on a larger scale. The stem, is however, broken off short, and the bowl is inserted into a holder or base, which also receives the new stem (Fig. 224). By this arrangement both bowl and stem are upright, and the pipe hangs down comfortably into the hand, while the deleterious juices of the tobacco (Pepys tells how he spent a pleasant afternoon at the Royal Society where it was shown that one drop of the juice killed a cat) drain naturally down into the holder and can never reach the mouth. Such a pipe is capable of infinite variations, in respect both of the decoration of the bowl, and the material (often a simple cherry-wood) and decoration of the stem. An elaborate example from the Dunhill collection

FIG. 224.— Typical Central European Pipe.

is shown in Plate XXIII. The bowl also is frequently fashioned from wood, as in the finely curved specimen from Bavaria shown in Plate XXIII. It will be noticed that the useless " spur " is still retained in such pipes, but it may move to the base or holder, as in the grotesque horn pipe from the Tyrol (Plate XXIII.), and disappears in the beautiful French porcelain pipes. The French makers excel in pipes of graceful design and execution, subjects of topical interest often being chosen. The portrait figure of Napoleon offers a fine example, as does that of the Crimean veteran (Plate XXIV.), and other portrait pipes are to be seen in the Dunhill collection.

FIG. 225.—Red Indian Pipe : Bowl in Cougar's Mouth.

Pottery and porcelain manufacturers have often been attracted by the pipe as a subject for their art, although many of the products are meant for ornament rather than for practical use. Such are the elaborate coiled or snake pipes of Staffordshire ware, of which some beautiful specimens are shown in Plate XXV. The device of a snake's head holding the bowl is reminiscent of Red Indian art (see

Fig. 225), and is seen again in a specimen in Plate XXVI. Even more attractive, although equally unpractical, are the coloured pipes of old Bristol glass, of which two unusually fine specimens are shown in Plate XXVII. Some beautiful pipes of Whieldon ware are shown in Plate XXVI.

The first pipe really to challenge the supremacy of the clay in England, and of the porcelain pipe in Central Europe, was the meerschaum. Meerschaum, or *l'écume de mer*, was so named from its likeness to petrified sea-foam, and the main source of the world's supply is Eskisher, in Asia Minor, a part of the Turkish Empire. The story runs that the first meerschaum pipe was made by a Hungarian shoemaker, Karl Kowates, two hundred years ago. Kowates, who lived at Budapest, was a skilled carver and made wooden pipes for his customers in his spare time. One day a certain Count Andrassy brought him a lump of meerschaum that had been presented to him in Turkey, and asked him to make a pipe of it. Kowates made not one, but two, keeping the second for his own use, and presently he discovered that where his fingers constantly touched the bowl the meerschaum had turned a beautiful golden brown. He realized that it was not his fingers, but the cobbler's wax with which they were constantly greased that had caused the change, so he waxed the whole pipe, and found that not only did it " colour " all over, but that it gave a sweeter smoke than before. Whether the story is true or not, the waxing process is essential to the manufacture of a meerschaum pipe, and this manufacture has always had its main centre in Austria-Hungary and particularly in artistic and luxury-loving Vienna. The bowls are shaped out roughly before they are exported from Turkey, and that is probably the reason why the typical meerschaum shape in its general outline and proportion resembles the bowl of a Turkish *chibouque*. This is seen by comparing the commonest pattern of meerschaum bowl sketched in Fig. 226 *a* with that of the Turkish bowl in Fig. 226 *b*. The bowls tend to be of large diameter and thick at the base, and are quite unlike the tall, slender

FIG. 226.—*a*, Typical Meerschaum Bowl; *b*, Turkish Pipe Bowl.

porcelain bowl of Central Europe, although many variations from the fundamental pattern may be found.

It is said that a meerschaum cannot be coloured to perfection if it is ever allowed to cool, and since there are moments, and even hours, when the most inveterate pipe-lover must lay his pipe aside, such perfection seems unattainable. An enthusiast of the fifties, however, hit upon the ingenious plan of arranging through his tobacconist for a detachment of lifeguardsmen to smoke his pipe in an endless chain so that it was always warm. Swaddled carefully in soft flannel, and filled always with the best tobacco at its owner's expense, the pipe passed from mouth to mouth for the space of seven months. When it was finally unwrapped, it was coloured a rich deep brown, pronounced perfect by connoisseurs of the art of pipe-colouring. But the aesthetic pleasure of the owner in his unique possession was somewhat dulled when the tobacconist presented him also with a bill for over one hundred pounds which had disappeared in smoke!

The ideal mouthpiece for a meerschaum pipe, cigar-holder, or cigarette-holder is one of amber, and consequently the working of amber became likewise centred at Vienna. Amber has a romantic history, for it is found almost exclusively on the Baltic coast of Prussia, and to a certain extent on the shores of the North Sea, and owing to its attractive and ornamental appearance has been a coveted possession since the dawn of history. The old "amber route," along which this semi-precious substance was traded from hand to hand from the northern barbarians to the civilized peoples of the Mediterranean Sea, probably passed through the site of modern Vienna, and that city has never been without its interest in amber. The magnificent pipe made entirely of amber, now in the Dunhill collection (Plate XXVII.), and once the property of a rich Chinese, is probably of Viennese work-manship.

The latter half of the seventeenth cen-tury, which saw the spread of the pipe into the remotest

FIG. 227.—Russian Pipe from Crimean Battlefield.

parts of Europe, was also the period of the greatest extension of the Turkish power, through and beyond the Balkan peninsula, and into the south of Russia. Hence it is not surprising that Russian pipes are reminiscent in shape, so far as the bowl is concerned, of the Turkish *chibouque*. The stem, however, is short, for the Russian peasant does not sit upon the floor, or lounge upon a divan, nor is he a man of leisure like the Turk. The Russian pipe is naturally of wood, for this is the material of which most of the utensils of these people are fash-

Fig. 228.—Finland Pipe: Russian Model.

ioned, since their original home was the forested country. The specimen sketched in Fig. 227, from the Dunhill collection, has the additional interest that it was brought from the field of battle by an officer fighting in the Crimean War.

The influence of the Russian pipe on those of Siberia has already been commented on, and that the pipes of Finland derive from those of Russia is

Fig. 229.—Pipe from Imatra: Finland.

suggested by the big wooden bowl of Finnish workmanship shown in the Dunhill collection (Fig. 228), and by the pipe from Imatra, collected by Mr. Bassett Digby, shown in Fig. 229. The latter has a mouthpiece of horn, and a flexible stem, which probably derived originally from Germany. Curved wooden stems are also used in Finland.

Bokhara and Khirghiz pipes are sketched for the

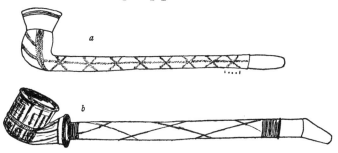

FIG. 230.—*a*, Kirghiz Pipe ; *b*, Bokhara Pipe.

sake of comparison (Fig. 230); they too are derived originally from Turkish pipes, and have stems that are long and straight, although not so long as that of a *chibouque*.

CHAPTER XIV

THE MODERN BRIAR

WHILE both clay and meerschaum pipes have the essential advantage of giving a cool, sweet smoke, their fragility is a drawback that must always remain insuperable. Metals, such as iron and silver, while certainly durable, conduct heat so rapidly that pipes of such material at once become too hot, while their weight too is a disadvantage. Wood, on the other hand, is light, durable, and a bad conductor of heat, and thus has three essential qualities of a good pipe material, but as an examination of native wooden pipes will reveal, most varieties of wood rapidly char and crack owing to the heat of the burning tobacco. The problem is thus to find some kind of wood which, while close-grained and heat-resistant, can yet be "turned" without too great difficulty. Cherry-wood has many of the required qualities, and is especially sweet-smoking, even from the first, but the interior of the bowl will never carbonize well and the wood

240

lends itself only to rough shaping. A certain amount of Australian Myall-wood is used in France, and some hard "Congo wood" at Vienna, but neither of these is widely popular. In Germany, before the coming of the meerschaum, the wooden pipes carved by the peasants of the Black Forest had a considerable vogue. These were made from the close-grained and gnarled root of the dwarf-oak, the wood being hard enough to resist fire, and charring very slowly. Such a use of *root* anticipates the wooden briar, as does, in cruder fashion, the countryman's gorse-root pipe already referred to and pictured (Fig. 8).

In the United States, the countrymen of a generation or two ago solved the pipe problem by the use of the corn-cob, the hard stem which bears the grains of maize, and that such a pipe gives a fairly satisfactory "smoke" is witnessed to by the fact that the making of corn-cob pipes is now an established factory industry. The great centre of production is Washington, a little town in Missouri, in the heart of the corn belt of the Middle West, and the neighbouring farmers make quite a profit by growing the extra-large cobs from which some twenty-seven million pipes are annually turned. The corn-cob pipe, however, like the English clay, is nowadays in use mainly among the humblest class of smokers, to whom cheapness is everything. It has, of course, followed the maize plant overseas, and may be seen between the lips of the Italian peasant, the South Africa Kaffir, and the Argentine *peon*.

The discovery of the ideal pipe material, the so-called briar-root, was quite accidental, as such discoveries so often are. It was incidental to the revival of the cult of the great Napoleon in the second decade following his death in 1821, when the disasters of 1814 were forgotten. Those who wished to honour their late Emperor were not content to visit the tomb at the Invalides, whither his ashes had been brought from St. Helena, but made a pilgrimage also to the birthplace of the Little Corporal in Corsica. Among these pilgrims was a French pipe-maker, who during his stay had the misfortune to break or lose his meerschaum pipe. He commissioned a Corsican peasant to carve him another, and this was done, the pipe proving such a success that its possessor secured a specimen of the wood from which it was made and brought it home with him. This wood, noted locally for its hardness and fine grain, was the root of the tree-heath, or bruyère, to give it its French

name, and from this date, somewhere in the early
fifties, it was destined to supersede all other pipe
materials. The specimen roots which the French
pipe-maker brought away from Corsica were sent
by him to a factory at St. Claude from which he was
accustomed to buy wooden pipe-stems, where it was
turned into bowls, and thus one more was added to
the already far-famed *articles de St. Claude.*

The history of this little town is a remarkable
one. Situated in a remote valley of the Jura
Mountains and hemmed in by forest-clad limestone ridges, its inhabitants look to their woods
and pastures as a means of livelihood. During the
winter season the heavy falls of snow make it
necessary to house the cattle, and out-of-door
work is impossible. Hence the winter days were
passed, as in the Alps and in Norway, in making all
sorts of articles for household use. At the great
Abbey, which was the nucleus of the settlement, the
monks occupied their enforced leisure in carving
and polishing rosary beads and other objects of
devotion, utilizing the box-wood which grew
abundantly in the neighbourhood. Box-wood
lends itself admirably to the turner's art, and the
well-made rosaries soon found a market outside the
Abbey walls at the country fair. The peasants

began to imitate the monks, producing a variety of useful articles—spigots, bobbins, snuff-boxes, basins and the like—in excess of their own needs, and adding pipe-stems to the list in the eighteenth century. Thus turnery became an established industry, and the young folk who had hitherto migrated to the plains and cities of France remained in the mountains. In consequence, the former village grew to a thriving little town, of which the Abbey church is now the cathedral. St. Claude stands, moreover, where two rushing torrents meet, and as the turnery grew from a home to a workshop industry, the streams were harnessed to turn the lathes and the polishing mops.

The fortunate accident that brought to the St. Claudians, with their age-old tradition of turnery, the first specimens of bruyère root, gave a fresh impetus to the growth of the town, and the manufacture of *la pipe* ousted that of the lesser wooden articles, which are now mainly confined to the surrounding villages. The new industry, however, did not come into existence without serious setbacks, for bruyère roots differ among themselves according to their age and the locality in which they grow, and they are so knotted and gnarled, and so often contain flaws, that it takes a very experienced worker to judge how to cut the root to advantage. The seasoning process is, moreover, a complex one. Yet once these initial difficulties were overcome, the new French briar gained steadily in reputation, and now no fewer than thirty million pipes are turned out from St. Claude in the course of a year, of which 90 per. cent. are exported, for the Frenchman himself has been, until quite recently, a devotee of the cigarette rather than of the pipe. The bulk of the St. Claude pipes come to England, which imports, according to official statistics, about twenty-five million pipes annually while exporting a quarter of a million superfine pipes of English make, besides twenty million English clays.

In accordance with the French policy of utilizing to the utmost the "white coal" of her mountain regions, a large electrical installation now supplies power to the pipe-factories, and these provide work for 5,000 people. This is a high proportion of a total of 14,000 inhabitants, but women as well as men are employed on a large scale, their work being to polish the bowls. Since the valley in which St. Claude stands is narrow, and the hill slopes are steep, building sites present a problem which is solved by the erection of very lofty buildings, so that the growth of the town is skywards after the fashion of New York.

The bruyère root is not confined to Corsica, but is indigenous to the whole margin of the Western Mediterranean, being specially adapted to the peculiar climatic régime of that area. An intensely dry, hot summer follows a mild and showery winter, and it is in the effort to pass successfully through the season of drought that the tree-heath has developed the huge, close-grained, deeply penetrating roots that give it its special value. The quality of the soil, too, is not without its influence, and the best roots are those that have thrust their way into the interstices of a rocky hillside. At present Calabria in Southern Italy, and Algeria, are the chief areas drawn upon, and since the heath is of very slow growth, there must come a day when the root will be scarce, and perhaps a substitute found. Nor is this all; the best roots are those that have died and been seasoned *in situ* and it is this "dead-root," broken in by Nature herself, that can never be artificially replaced.

The making of articles in horn was always a subsidiary industry of the cattle-keeping people of the Jura, so that from the first, horn pipe-stems were locally manufactured, with stems of amber and ivory for the "pipe de luxe." But with the increasing popularity of the briar, the demand for a really cheap yet efficient mouthpiece became imperative, and the ebonite or vulcanite mouth-piece was devised by an English firm in 1878. As has so often been the case in respect of English dis-coveries, the Germans, with their superior technical knowledge and equipment, took over the invention and brought it to a perfection that ensured them a practical monopoly of the output. Not long before the war, however, a small factory for making these mouthpieces was set up in St. Claude, and when the German supplies were cut off, this little business expanded to meet not only the demand for pipe-stems, but the even more pressing demand for ebonite parts essential to electrical apparatus. Now, of course, the French industry is firmly established, and the German monopoly is broken.

Of the prehistoric smokers of the Far East we are but dimly aware, nor do any of their pipes remain. A thousand years of Indian smoking in America saw the evolution of pipes, which were sometimes elaborate, but always clumsy, fashioned as they were for the most part of coarse pottery or stone. The pipe-makers of Europe, early discarding the Indian models, have had well-nigh four hundred years to bring their art to perfection, and the perfection they have achieved is that of simplicity. Elaborately decorated and mounted pipes, like pipes of uncouth shape and size, have had their day, save among the young and the semi-barbaric. The twentieth-century connoisseur selects his pipe of self-seasoned bruyère and plain vulcanite for the excellence of its workmanship, the correctness of its proportions, and, above all, for the delicate beauty of its flawless, straight-grained bowl.

INDEX

NOTE.—*The references in heavy black numerals indicate illustrations in the text.*